HISTORIC HOUSES
OF THE
SOUTH

SOUTHERN ACCENTS PRESS

HISTORIC HOUSES

OF THE

SOUTH

Simon and Schuster
New York

FRONTISPIECE
The music room at the Richardson-Owens-Thomas House in Savannah, Georgia.

PAGE vi (Opposite Introduction)
The wide avenue of live oaks leading to Live Oak Plantation in West Feliciana Parish, Louisiana.

This book consists of revised and enlarged essays originally published in SOUTHERN ACCENTS magazine.

Published by Simon and Schuster, a Division of Simon & Schuster, Inc., Simon & Schuster Building, Rockefeller Center,
1230 Avenue of the Americas, New York, New York 10020

SIMON AND SCHUSTER and colophon are registered trademarks of Simon & Schuster, Inc.

Manufactured in Italy

First Printing 1984
1 2 3 4 5 6 7 8 9 10
Library of Congress Cataloging in Publication Data
ISBN: 0-671-52691-X

CONTENTS

INTRODUCTION

SOUTHERN ACCENTS, subtitled "The Magazine of Fine Southern Interiors and Gardens," began as a dream back in 1977. It was a dream that had substance. Today, in 1984, the magazine is a recognizable part of American culture and has found a welcoming readership not only in the South but also throughout the nation as a whole.

Since we began publishing SOUTHERN ACCENTS, we have noticed a very high degree of interest among our readers in homes that have historic provenance . . . and there are many such homes in the South. This book is a celebration of twenty of these, built from 1730 to 1908, and selected by the editors for their special charm and history.

SOUTHERN ACCENTS takes as its editorial province the old Confederacy, plus certain contiguous states and the District of Columbia. We limit our coverage to the following: Alabama, Tennessee, Georgia, Florida, Mississippi, North Carolina, South Carolina, Virginia, West Virginia, Arkansas, Louisiana, Kentucky, Maryland, Texas and Washington, D.C. It is because of our concentration on this particular area of the United States that the publication has found its niche.

And the words "particular area" are carefully chosen. The South is particular — some even say peculiar — and very different from other regions of the country. It's a nation within a nation, one that once tried desperately to become an entity unto itself. W.J. Cash, in his monumental work "The Mind of the South"* offers the lyrical description of Southern society before all was gone with the wind:

"What the Old South of the legend in its classical form was like is more or less familiar to everyone. It was a sort of stage piece out of the eighteenth century, wherein gesturing gentlemen moved soft-spokenly against a background of rose gardens and dueling grounds, through always gallant deeds, and lovely ladies, in farthingales, never for a moment lost that exquisite remoteness which has been the dream of all men and the possession of none. Its social pattern was manorial, its civilization that of the Cavalier, its ruling class an aristocracy coextensive with the planter group — men often entitled to quarter the royal arms of St. George and St. Andrew on their shields, and in every case descended from the old gentlefolk who for many centuries had made up the ruling classes of Europe.

"They dwelt in large and stately mansions, preferably white and with columns and Grecian entablature . . . their social life [was] a thing of old world splendor and delicacy. What had really happened here, indeed, was that the gentlemanly idea, driven from England by Cromwell, had taken refuge in the South and fashioned for itself a world to its heart's desire: a world singularly polished and mellow and poised, wholly dom-inated by ideals of honor and chivalry and *noblesse* — all those sentiments and values and habits of action which used to be, especially in Walter Scott, invariably assigned to the gentleman born and the Cavalier . . .

". . . Here, indeed, there was a genuine, if small, aristocracy. Here was all that in aftertime was to give color to the legend of the Old South. Here were silver and carriages and courtliness and manner. Here were great houses — not as great as we are sometimes told, but still great houses: the Shirleys, the Westovers, the Stratfords. Here were the names that were some time to flash with swords and grow tall in thunder — the Lees, the Stuarts and the Beauregards . . ."

The New South has long since heeded General Robert E. Lee's advice to the distraught widow of a Confederate soldier after the War Between the States had reached its bloody end: "Madam, do not train up your children in hostility to the government of the United States. Remember, we are all one country now . . . bring them up to be Americans."

Americans we all are now. But memories of the Old South still haunt, and the twenty homes presented herewith conjure them up. They range from a Virginia plantation to a Carolina tidewater tabby house and deeper South to the resplendent Greek Revival Mansions of the Cotton Kings.

Half of the houses presented are privately owned by people who have put forth enormous effort and prodigious amounts of time and money to restore them as authentically as possible. Some of these private homes accept special tours on occasion; others are open only to the discreet eye of the camera of SOUTHERN ACCENTS. The other ten are of the public domain and open to public touring on a regular basis. Most are on the National Register of Historic Places; all bear witness to the dedication of preservationists who have raised America's awareness to the precariousness of our precious heritage.

I am very proud of the work our staff has done in preparing HISTORIC HOUSES OF THE SOUTH. We intend this to be the first in a series of books of this genre . . . books which we feel will find themselves welcome in the libraries of readers throughout the nation.

Walter Mitchell Jr.

Walter Mitchell, Jr.
Publisher, SOUTHERN ACCENTS

*From THE MIND OF THE SOUTH, by W. J. Cash. Copyright 1941 by Alfred A. Knopf, Inc., and renewed 1969 by Mary R. Maury. Reprinted by permission of the publisher.

HISTORIC HOUSES

OF THE

SOUTH

STRATFORD HALL

Stratford Hall, a national shrine for half a century, is a heroic memorial worthy of the illustrious family that first owned and occupied it — the Lees of Virginia. Overlooking the Potomac River in Westmoreland County, Virginia, this historic 18th century home was designed as part of a self-sufficient plantation complex, almost a sovereign community unto itself.

The Hall was built by Thomas Lee and was the birthplace of six of his eight children, among them Richard Henry Lee and Francis Lightfoot Lee. It was also home to Thomas' great-nephew Henry (Light-Horse Harry) Lee, whose own son Robert E. Lee became the most revered general of the Confederacy.

This dashing family was prominent in America's early development, producing judges, governors, lawmakers, educators, planters, military men and ambassadors.

Just as unique as the family that graced its environs, Stratford Hall is remarkable as a forthright, distinctive variation of the Georgian style. Its formal, elegant design mandates its place among the great mansions of the nation.

The Lee chronicle began at Stratford Hall in 1716 when Thomas Lee, newly wed to Hannah Ludwell, bought the land from the widow of Nathaniel Pope and some years later began construction on a bluff above the Potomac River.

Ninety feet from east to west, the main house of Stratford was designed in the shape of an "H," a massive center block forming the middle crossbar and matching strong rectangular-shaped wings on either side. Also known as the "Great House," this structure was in turn served by four outlying dependencies constructed at equal distances from each of its four corners. The north front faces the river; the south side overlooks a wall dividing the manicured lawn adjacent to the house from grazing pasture and meadow beyond.

The roof line of the "Great House" is graced by eight tall brick chimneys. Grouped together in a square-shaped cluster of four on each of the two wings, they are connected at their top by brick arches and at the hipped roof line by a wooden platform and balustrades. The effect when seen from a distance is of two towers anchoring the east and west wings, respectively, each providing a lookout vantage for the river traffic below.

The "Great House" is two-storied and, with the exception of the two rooms located in the connecting crossbar section, every room has its own corner view.

Situated in the middle crossbar section of the "H" is the large counting room and above it, the great hall, distinguished as one of the most beautiful rooms in America. It was planned as a reception/ballroom and was used for the stunning entertainment center of the house. Twenty-nine feet square, with a 17-foot-high tray ceiling, its walls are adorned with applied pilasters and ornately carved Corinthian capitals. There are no fireplaces, and its furnishings were kept close to the walls leaving the center free for dancing. Double doors open out on both sides of the great hall, offering limitless views of the river to the north and meadows to the south.

Thomas Lee, the builder of this manse, was as distinguished as any of his more famous descendants. At the age of 23, he was heir to a brilliant mind and an industrious spirit. Building upon his father's and grandfather's successes, Thomas was to become Justice of Westmoreland, a member of the House of Burgesses, a naval officer of the Potomac and agent for the Proprietary of the Northern Neck. He was appointed to His Majesty's Council in 1732, negotiated with the Iroquois Indians, founded The Ohio Company and in the late 1740's, was made chief executive of the Virginia Colony.

At his parents' death, Philip, the eldest of Thomas' children, inherited Stratford Hall. He, too, was a member of the Council and House of Burgesses and, even more ambitious for the property than his father, he initiated a gristmill and shipbuilding yard at the landing and began breeding horses. Philip's imported English stallion "Dotterel" gave a glorious beginning to Stratford's establishment as one of the great American Thoroughbred stud farms in the Rappahannock Valley. In the years immediately preceding the Revolutionary War, Philip remained loyal to the Crown, but his brothers helped lead the Colonies to independence: Richard Henry, six years younger than his brother, Philip, was also a member of the House of Burgesses and a delegate to the First Continental Congress in 1774; his younger brother, Francis Lightfoot, was a delegate to the Second Congress. Richard Henry was one of the framers of the Declaration of Independence, and both he and Francis Lightfoot were signers.

Stratford passed from Philip and his wife Elizabeth Steptoe to his daughter, Matilda Lee, who had married her spirited cousin, Henry Lee, dubbed "Light-Horse Harry" for his dashing raids as a part of the Continental Army. Henry was elected to the Virginia House of Delegates, the Continental Congress and served three terms as Governor of Virginia. After Matilda died, leaving him heartbroken and alone with three small children, Henry married Ann Hill Carter. His poor business speculations led to his loss of fortune, and when Henry and Ann's fifth child, Robert E. Lee, was only a toddler, his father was led ignominiously away to debtors' prison. At Henry's death, the mansion was inherited by Henry Lee IV, his son by his first wife, Matilda.

Henry Lee, a legislator and soldier like his father, fell heir to a great house sorely neglected and in need of repair. Marrying well to Anne McCarty, whose dowry helped finance necessary improvements, he was unfortunately involved in a scandal with Anne's sister, Elizabeth, and later financial difficulties related to the affair forced him to sell Stratford to a friend, William Clarke Somerville. Ironically, the Hall was later sold at auction to Henry Storke and his wife, Elizabeth McCarty Storke, the same sister-in-law who had so influenced Henry's downfall; the Storkes were to live at Stratford Hall for the next 50 years.

In 1929, Ethel Armes and May Field Lanier raised $240,000 to buy the deteriorating mansion. Fiske Kimball of Philadelphia was commissioned to oversee the restoration. Stratford's interior walls and woodwork were lovingly restored to their original colors. While few pieces of the Lees' furniture remain, the present furnishings are based on inventories taken from the records of Thomas and Philip Lee, and none is dated later than 1810. The Robert E. Lee Memorial Association, organized by Mrs. Lanier, dedicated Stratford Hall to the public in 1935.

PRECEDING PAGES. *Stratford Hall, an imposing Georgian country house in Westmoreland County, Virginia, was built by Thomas Lee between 1725 and 1730. Although architectural historians argue the origin of Stratford's H-shape plan, it stands as a monument to the illustrious Lees' of Virginia who lived within its walls for so many years.*

LEFT. *Large doors open into the great hall, which has a ceiling height of 17 feet. Corinthian pilasters reinforce the architectural wood paneling of pine, poplar and gum, which are painted the original color. The Chippendale sofa was made by Jonathan Gostelowe of Philadelphia, circa 1770; chairs on either side of a Queen Anne walnut tea table are Philadelphia Chippendale. On the table in the foreground is a large salver supported by three scroll and shell feet. It bears the Lee crest of a squirrel eating an acorn and was made by Ebenezer Coker, London 1736.*

FACING PAGE. *The dining room closet features a portrait of Queen Caroline, wife of George II. The Queen Anne gateleg table holds a pair of English rococo shell base candlesticks and Chinese export porcelain. The rug is an Oushak.*

ABOVE. *The parlor next to the great hall was enlarged and remodeled into the Federal style about 1790. Light-Horse Harry Lee's portrait by Gilbert Stuart hangs above the fireplace mantel, which holds a Chinese export porcelain garniture. Standing in front of the tall clock made by Jonathan Johnson, London, circa 1770, is a very fine tilt and turn table from Philadelphia. The Hepplewhite breakfront secretary, 1790-1800 made in Salem, Massachusetts, belonged to General Robert E. Lee. The Chippendale gaming table holds rococo silver candlesticks crafted by James Gould, London, 1746. The rug is Aubusson.*

LEFT. *A wide arch unites the dining room with the dining room closet. The English Queen Anne mahogany dining table is set with part of a service imported from China about 1790. Pistol handled knives, rat-tail spoons and three tined forks are 18th century; Chippendale baroque candlesticks were crafted by William Cafe, London, 1762.*

ABOVE. *Four generations of Lees were born in the mother's room, including two signers of the Declaration of Independence, Richard Henry and Francis Lightfoot Lee, and in 1807, Robert E. Lee who led the Confederate Army. A leather and iron trunk studded with brass, circa 1790, sits at the foot of the canopied Sheraton mahogany bed. The Lee family American walnut crib, draped in mosquito netting, stands before the window.*

RIGHT. *The Massachusetts Chippendale block front chest-on-chest is adorned with a molded broken arch scroll top and three spiral finials, circa 1770. The japanned red lacquer embroidery frame is English, circa 1725.*

FACING PAGE. *The nursery adjoining the mother's room is furnished with a child's arched tester field bed hung in white dimity, the doll's bed beside it is draped to match. Toys, including an 18th century wooden horse on wheels, date from the period of the Lees' occupancy.*

ABOVE. *The kitchen is separate from the great hall as were most kitchens on Southern plantations. A large cooking fireplace dominates the room whose furniture and utensils date from the 18th century. Three steps lead to a warming oven, the cooking oven is inside the right wall of the fireplace.*

RIGHT. *The kitchen yard contains a wellhouse and a huge copper kettle suspended from a tripod for cooking and washing. Herbs such as mint, sage, chives, thyme, rosemary, parsley and others grow around the perimeter.*

FACING PAGE. *A decorative gate opens onto the rolling meadow outside the formal garden revealing an octagonal garden house in the background.*

DRAYTON HALL

In a region of impressive, time-honored houses, Drayton Hall stands apart. It remains almost unchanged after 242 years, a majestic, authoritative statement of the fine reach and grasp of America's early builders.

Located on the Ashley River near Charleston, South Carolina, the mansion was completed in 1742 after four years of careful and painstaking labor. Its architect is unknown, but his work reveals an educated and practiced eye, clearly aware of the Renaissance influences of Andrea Palladio. Although the popularity of Palladian style was much in evidence in mid-18th century Britain, the beauty of line captured at Drayton Hall has rarely been equaled or interpreted more handsomely.

In 1796, just 54 years after its completion, the visiting Duke de La Rochefoucault-Liancourt dismissed Drayton Hall offhandedly as "an ancient building, but convenient and good." Nonetheless, the Duke was moved to admire its gardens as "better laid out, better cultivated and stocked with good trees, than any I have hitherto seen."

Drayton Hall is not kept as a furnished residence. The great house, preserved by the National Trust For Historic Preservation, stands without embellishment, its imposing lines unsoftened by blandishment of fabrics, furnishings, floor coverings, cabinetry or accessories. It has neither electricity nor gas, central heat nor plumbing. Some of its surfaces have never been repainted, and little rejuvenation has been done in the 20th century. Only a compelling landmark could stand in such austerity and continue to draw students of art, architecture, history and landscaping to acclaim its profound architectural significance and hordes of visitors honoring it as a splendid example of Carolina Low Country design.

John Drayton, whose father Thomas Drayton came to South Carolina from Barbados in 1679, purchased the original Drayton land for £ 3,500 in 1738. Construction of his home began shortly, and although neither an architect nor a builder has ever been identified, it seems clear that the designer had access to contemporary design manuals. Evidence of this is furnished by at least one overmantel in the great hall downstairs which bears a direct reference to a pattern found in William Kent's *Designs of Inigo Jones* published in 1727. Specific debts to the influences of Palladio and Jones can be seen throughout much of the interior; the exterior architectural style is dedicated to the Palladian concepts of symmetry, order and classical form.

The Portland stone for the portico was imported from England, but the brick, laid in Flemish bond, the structural pine and the decorative cypress paneling all came from local sources. Two flanking wings were added within 20 years after the main building's completion.

John Drayton, master of Drayton Hall, was married four times and had nine children. He was a member of the Royal Council to the Governor and Justice of the Court of Common Pleas until the outbreak of the Revolutionary War. His son, William Henry, was the author of a pamphlet signed "Freeman" that included a bill of rights and outlined a course of action that was to be substantially adopted by the newly formed Congress. In 1778, he was elected as a delegate to the Continental Congress but died a year later. Following in William Henry's footsteps, his son John Drayton was also politically active. He was instrumental in founding the University of South Carolina and was appointed to a two-year term as Lieutenant Governor and was then elected Governor for another two-year term.

Drayton Hall itself passed through seven generations to successive descendants. Included among them were doctors, jurists, horticulturists, botanists, government leaders, and always, planters. In the years preceding the Civil War, the house was used seasonally because of the vagaries of climate and planting rotations. Family diaries written before 1820 point to repeated maintenance efforts, especially to the leaking slate roof, which endangered interior plaster and wood. Reference is also made to items purchased in the 1800's and found listed in family inventories. They are an indication of the level of taste and culture prevalent in the Drayton home: a "grand Forte piano," a "Barbarini" vase, a mahogany "Duchesse" set and a mahogany "sopha bed" with bolster and tester.

During the financially depressed years following the Civil War, the main structure was often left unoccupied for long periods of time, its lands tenanted and watched over by families of former slaves. Corn was planted up to the stone steps, sheep cropped the grass leading to the river, and the estate occasionally became a refuge for squatters. These desperate days ended when the lands were leased for mining phosphates that had been discovered during the mid-1800's. By the 1880's, the Draytons were once again financially secure. Although they could now well afford extensive renovations, they chose instead to simply and dutifully maintain, preferring to build another mansion in peninsular Charleston in 1885.

The house had survived a great hurricane in 1813 and, in 1886, a severe earthquake that shocked the area, destroying the west wing flanker and damaging the plasterwork and ceilings in the main structure. The east flanker was ruined in the subsequent hurricane of 1893 and was then torn down. Although Victorian-era additions were constructed in the 1880's, repairs were limited to insuring the structure's survival and continued use of the house.

In this manner, brightened only by infrequent gala celebrations, the great house slumbered into the 20th century, cherished by its owners and the object of curiosity and occasional vandalism by sightseers. In 1974, the Draytons' pride in their ancestral home led to its final sale. Through the concerted efforts of the Historic Charleston Foundation, the State of South Carolina, the Department of Interior, the National Trust and private donors, it stands today as a national masterpiece, its architectural proportions and detail preserved, its purity of style intact.

FACING PAGE. *Drayton Hall is one of the finest Georgian mansions in North America. Begun in 1738, it lies outside Charleston, South Carolina, along the Ashley River. The west front or land side of the plantation house has two parallel stone staircases that lead to a double portico topped with a triangular pediment. Columns are Roman Doric on the first level and Ionic on the second; the roof is bell-cast with a flat top.*

ABOVE. *From the east or river side of the house, the lofty, mahogany paneled stair hall leads into the great halls on both the first and second floors.*

RIGHT. *The handcarved mahogany festoon over the window is unique among surviving American houses of this period. From the placement of detail, it is obvious that no allowance was made for window hangings. A panel directly to the left of the window is one of two shutters that folded across the window for protection.*

BELOW. *The ceiling, which dates from the time of construction, is one of the finest of its kind in America today. Its design was worked into wet plaster by a freehand technique.*

FACING PAGE, TOP LEFT. *Seen from the stair hall, the splendid fireplace in the great hall bears a striking similarity to the one in William Kent's* Designs of Inigo Jones, 1727. *Pilasters support the mantelshelf and the paterae in the cornice are repeated in the guilloche pattern on the overmantel.*

FACING PAGE, TOP RIGHT. *An elaborate doorway opens from the great hall into the stair hall. Walls in most of the rooms were painted blue toward the end of the 19th century.*

FACING PAGE, BOTTOM. *The river side of the house conforms to the Palladian idea of balance and order.*

19

TRYON PALACE

Tryon Palace of North Carolina, designed to be the most beautiful building in Colonial America, was fated from its beginning by unfortunate timing. Destined to be the home of the Royal Governor, the magnificent Palace was built in New Bern, then capital of the "Old North State," in a distinctive and fashionable English style which unfortunately became a symbol of British authority at the very moment the American colonies were rising toward rebellion against the crown. Fronting the Trent River, with a grand sweep of landscaped grounds leading to the water's edge, the Georgian residence became the bitter focus of desperate colonial taxpayers rankled by the yoke of monarchy.

After the Revolutionary War, the humbled Palace ceased to have an official function. It fell into indifferent hands and was burned. All that remained was one dependency. The rest was brick and ashes until the generous benefactions of two women, a mother and her daughter, spurred its reconstruction.

Now, splendidly restored and exquisitely furnished, the sumptuous Tryon Palace reigns as a national ornament.

Arriving in the American colonies in 1764, English architect John Hawks was well-prepared for his mission. He was traveling in the company of Lieutenant Colonel William Tryon and family. Colonel Tryon was to take office as Royal Governor of North Carolina, and as his first order of business, he had chosen young Hawks to design and oversee construction of their Colonial Palace at New Bern.

The assignment was the most important of his career, and Hawks had already done extensive research and preliminary drawings for the project. Together, Tryon and Hawks had decided that the edifice was to follow the Georgian style, the latest architectural fashion of London. This design choice was central to their vision of a structure that would represent the mother country, displaying a proud heritage for all to see.

Within weeks of their arrival, however, and even as the new governor called the General Assembly in session to outline plans for the capitol, news came that the British Parliament had passed the repugnant Stamp Act. This measure, added to the other growing grievances of the colonists, aroused instant antagonism to his plan.

Despite loud cries of discontent and the furious controversy that ensued, Tryon pressed his program. The Assembly, requiring additional revenues from constituents who had no interest in a project they considered ridiculous, was persuaded to vote £15,000 for the building. Special taxes that were levied to support its construction became a galling and unwelcome burden on the backwoodsmen and farmers of the district, and the structure, which was to be a "public ornament, a lasting monument to the liberality of the colony," was doomed in the minds of the local populace from its inception.

Tryon chose a site on the banks of the Trent for the complex, and Hawks sent final drawings of his plan to England for the crown's approval. Under his able direction, carpenters, carvers and stucco workers began work. He sent to London for skilled plumbers and to Philadelphia for other special craftsmen. Windows and mantels arrived from England, and within three years, the main building was ready for Governor Tryon and his family to occupy.

With the royal coat of arms emblazoned on a pediment, and life-size portraits of King George I, King George III and Queen Charlotte looking down at the gathering, the Palace was opened with a gala ceremony. At least one brave assemblyman managed to rise and praise the elegant and noble building, but the mood of the uninvited public was more in keeping with the political climate.

As the Townshend Acts were added to other repressive tax measures, the colonists became dangerously defiant. Stung by what he considered personal rejection, Tryon petitioned London to transfer him to the governorship of New York.

Tryon's successor, Josiah Martin, filled the Palace with a large family and an even larger appetite for the trappings of nobility. Sending to London for services of silver plate, a state coach and additional furniture, his grand lifestyle did nothing to endear him, or his seat of power, to the restless colonists chafing under his control. Within the span of a few years, Martin fled for his life from these same American patriots, and his last view of the Palace came from under cover of darkness as he slipped unobtrusively past the pigeon house and outbuildings to a waiting ship offshore.

The Revolutionary War had begun, and the once elegant Palace fell on hard times. Although confiscated by the state, the building was later abandoned, its lead gutters and iron palisades removed by the military to be melted down for bullets, the townspeople taking whatever else they could use. In 1798, while the structure was again briefly occupied by a local schoolmaster, sparks from a servant's torch lighted a fire that burned the Palace to the ground.

More than 125 years later, the Daughters of the Revolution, New Bern historians and school children began to urge a "regenerated Phoenix" campaign. A Tryon Palace Commission was established, and the North Carolina legislature appropriated $227,000 to purchase the lots of the original square complex and to remove the 54 buildings that had subsequently been constructed on the site. Through the generosity of Mrs. James Edwin Latham and her daughter Mrs. John A. Kellenberger, a trust fund was established for the Tryon Palace project and the reconstruction began.

The late William G. Perry, whose firm restored Colonial Williamsburg, was appointed architect, and under the direction of historian Alonzo T. Dill, the monumental and painstaking work of interpreting John Hawks' original drawings was begun. Spurred by the additional gift of Mrs. Latham's magnificent American and English antiques collection, period furnishings for the Palace interior were assembled and authenticated. Horticulturist Morley Jeffers Williams created the lovely gardens that grace the slopes surrounding the restored mansion.

In April 1959, the "Capitol Building on the Continent of North America" was again opened to the public — a superb monument to the 18th century men who designed and built it, and a lasting tribute to the 20th century men and women who had the vision to restore it.

FACING PAGE. *Tryon Palace was built in 1770 on the banks of the Trent River in New Bern, North Carolina, by British Royal Governor, William Tryon, as the capitol and governors residence of that Royal Colony. It burned to the ground in 1798, but was reconstructed and restored to its former glory in the 20th century.*

ABOVE. *Marble fragments found during excavation on the site indicated the use of white Italian and black Belgian marble in the entrance hall of the palace. Statues in the niches are 18th century marble figures representing the four continents.*

ABOVE. *The rich ochre color used on the walls of the library was determined by archeological finds on the site before restoration was begun. Prominent among the fine antiques are an English mirror in a gilt frame with brass candle holders which hangs above a carved mahogany kneehold desk. The unusual walnut roundabout chair is inlaid with bone.*

RIGHT. *The library holds first editions of 400 of the same books owned by Governor and Mrs. Tryon. The painting above the mantel is an architectural seascape of the school of Claude Lorrain. On the back wall is a portrait of Philip Bowes Broke, circa 1755, thought to be the earliest Thomas Gainsborough in America.*

LEFT. *Full length portraits of King George III and his concort, Queen Charlotte flanking the council Chamber mantel are by the school of Sir Joshua Reynolds. Matching mahogany tables with Gothic Chippendale chairs stand on a 17th century Isphahan carpet.*

ABOVE. *A silver inkstand, London, circa 1764, by William Plummer and silver candlesticks, London, circa 1720, by Richard Greene, rest on a Chippendale mahogany table desk.*

FACING PAGE. *Above the mantel in the dining room is an 18th century portrait of Mary Queen of Scots. Beneath an English cutglass chandelier, circa 1750, an Adam-Chippendale table surrounded by Chippendale chairs is set with a silver épergne centerpiece and Worcester porcelain. The Philadelphia tall-case clock case is 18th century.*

ABOVE. *Governor Tryon's bedroom displaying a large, four-poster canopied bed with French embroideried spread, reflects the tastes of a wealthy 18th century gentleman. The mantel and overmantel are English; the seascape is Dutch. In the corner is a Queen Anne bonnet top highboy in burl walnut from Massachusetts, circa 1735.*

LEFT. *In the upstairs family supper room, a Chinoiserie mirror with fanciful painting of an Oriental port hangs above a mahogany sofa which is covered with the original needlework.*

BACHELOR'S
BARTER

Bachelor's Barter is a stone house which was a fortress for pioneer living in the Kentucky wilderness of the late 1700's. Shaded by ancient trees and secluded behind rock-wall fences, the dwelling stands proudly amid bluegrass pastures just a few miles from Harrodsburg.

In recent years, the rugged, thick-walled house has had the rare good fortune to-fall into the hands of one of the most respected and experienced historians in the nation, James Lowry Cogar, who was involved in the Shaker Village restoration. The first, and for more than 30 years, curator at Colonial Williamsburg, Mr. Cogar was shown the honest old structure, acquired it, renamed it, oversaw its restoration, deeded it for preservation to Shaker Village of Pleasant Hill, Kentucky, and now lives in it as a cherishing tenant.

Freshened by its own spring-fed creek murmuring softly past its doors and furnished with fastidious integrity and exactitude, Bachelor's Barter now has star billing as an honest, endearing reflection of rustic progress in early America.

The structural genealogy of Bachelor's Barter has been as carefully traced as the Thoroughbred bloodlines of Kentucky's famous racing stables. Originally the home of Samuel Taylor, a man with many ties to the legal profession, the house contains an inscribed millstone above the front entrance lintel with the pragmatic, if unsentimental admonition, "Look to your Laws rather than to your progenitors for your inheritance," and the year "1790" marked at its base.

But the 1790 date has been questioned by restoration architects. The earliest section of the house consists of a two and one-half story white limestone building laid in broken ashlar pattern, one-room deep. Researchers now believe that architectural details, such as bold, raised-panel doors and the wide chair rail in the upper story, point to a construction date as early as 1782. The millstone, they reason, was put in place some years after the construction of the house was completed. Support for this later placement theory is indicated by surrounding stones that have been rudely cut to receive the millstone.

If the proper date of 1782 is taken instead of 1790, those would have been pivotal years indeed in the history of Kentucky, which was then wresting its separation from Virginia as its own state, and for Captain Samuel Taylor, a young man who was to play an important role during that period. A man of considerable consequence, he came to Kentucky from Cumberland County, Virginia, in 1779, and was named one of the trustees for the community of Harrodsburg, the first town in the Commonwealth of Kentucky. The Captain later served as the town surveyor, was elected to represent Mercer County in the Virginia legislature and served three terms as a state representative after Kentucky became a state.

In 1780, Colonel Stephen Trigg, a Virginia native who originally came to Kentucky as a member of the Virginia Land Commission, established a station of 4000 acres of land in eastern Mercer County. In late 1781, he sold to Captain Samuel Taylor 600 acres along a branch of Shawnee Run Creek, and the structure Taylor subsequently built on this property has the undocumented distinction of being sometimes mistakenly identified as Trigg's Station. Although the site of Trigg's own 1780 homestead is southeast of the property he conveyed to the Captain in 1781, the misnomer stuck.

Located on a tributary of the Shawnee, Samuel Taylor built his house facing southward. It had center doors, front and back, and three nine-over-six light sash on the first floor, and three six-over-six light sash at the upper level. Massive chimneys anchored the house at both gable ends.

In 1811, Taylor sold his farm to his son-in-law John Glover, and two brick wings were added. The first two-story wing was placed on the east side of the original structure, with a doorway cut through the heavy stone wall on the first level only. This two-level addition was one-room wide on the main floor and was used as a parlor or morning room. A second one-story wing was attached at a stepped-down elevation to the north of the morning room and consisted of two rooms: a dining room, and beyond it, a large kitchen. Window frames with spaced reeding and carved rosettes in the corner blocks are the most notable architectural features of the brick wings and are attributed to a well-known Mercer County master builder, Matthew Lowrey.

In 1900, D.B. Chatham purchased the old Taylor home and farm from John and Jane Huguely. Some years later, the property passed into the hands of Mrs. Lily Higginbotham, and the history of its subsequent transfer to Mr. Cogar explains why the house he dubbed "Bachelor's Barter" accurately describes both his marital status and the manner in which it was acquired.

When Mr. Cogar decided to return from Williamsburg to his native Kentucky to direct the restoration of Shaker Village, an ingenious swap of property was seen as a mutual advantage by all parties. Colonial Williamsburg purchased the old Taylor house and 194 acres of farmland from Mrs. Higginbotham to exchange it with Mr. Cogar for historic property he owned in Williamsburg, consisting of a distinguished house, an 18th-century shop building and a large lot on York Street. Once the barter was completed, Mr. Cogar engaged Washington Reed of Warrenton, Virginia, as architect for the restoration of his newly acquired Kentucky dwelling.

A skilled crew of craftsmen was employed in June 1964, and by autumn, the work was finished. Mr. Cogar chose the garret for his bedroom suite, adding dormer windows for light and ventilation. Uncovered during the renovation was an underground passage that had at one time connected the cellar kitchen with the log springhouse and provided the early frontier settlers with a secure and easily accessible water supply in case of Indian attack. A new kitchen, with beaded board cabinets, brick floor and a large cooking fireplace now in place, is where Mr. Cogar, raconteur and chef of great repute, converses and cooks with flair.

In deeding his residence to Shaker Village, James Cogar has assured the preservation of this wonderful and historic legacy. Of equal consequence, a lifetime collection of English and American furniture and accessories, amassed by one of the nation's foremost authorities on period antiques, has found a perfect home in Bachelor's Barter.

LEFT. *A portion of the 18th century stone fence still stands before Bachelor's Barter, one of Kentucky's early stone houses, nestled in a valley six miles from Harrodsburg. The log springhouse is connected to the cellar of the main house by an underground passageway. In earlier days, the tunnel provided access to fresh water in the event of an Indian attack.*

ABOVE. *When summer cover replaces heavier, winter decoration, Oriental rugs give way to straw mats in the living room and elsewhere in the house. A needlepoint pillow depicting the barter of Cogar's Williamsburg house in exchange for Bachelor's Barter rests on a mahogany Chippendale armchair with pierced splat. A mahogany concertina table is placed before an English mahogany Chippendale sofa, and a globe on a tripod stand is exhibited near the fireplace. A Chippendale mahogany barometer, circa 1770, hangs on the wall. Engraver J. Barney's London print, entitled* The Fisherman Returns, *hangs above the fireplace.*

The morning room offers a comfortable conversational setting. A walnut Queen Anne fiddle-back armchair and a Chippendale mahogany wing chair, circa 1770, are seen at the left; a Scottish mahogany tripod tier table of the same period stands to the right of the fireplace. A Queen Anne walnut side chair is placed before an American applewood secretary, circa 1770. In front of the sofa is a 19th century English horse racing game with satinwood board, painted lead horses and riders, counters and ivory dice. Seth Thomas mantel clock dates around 1810.

LEFT. *Blue Canton porcelains provide colorful accents in the handsome dining room. A primitive portrait from Mr. Cogar's family hangs above the late 18th century applewood sideboard, and a small applewood side table stands in front of the window. The late 18th century applewood drop-leaf dining table is set with Oriental export china, German pewter fluted column candlesticks and English air twist wineglasses. An Irish brass and glass lantern, circa 1780, hangs above. The armchair and side chairs are late 18th century.*

ABOVE. *A late 18th century American corner cupboard in the dining room displays Oriental export china.*

LEFT. *The kitchen features a capacious fireplace and basket weave brick floor. An English pine shelf hangs over the limestone lintel, and a butler stand is used near the stair. Welsh side chairs with pierced slats are drawn up to the applewood drop-leaf table. A Windsor bench with arrow spindles, circa 1820, faces the fireplace.*

TOP. *The design for the twin tester bed in the guest bedroom was adapted from an 18th century double bed that Mr. Cogar donated to Colonial Williamsburg.*

ABOVE. *An English tin lantern hangs above a drop-leaf applewood table on the summer porch. A pine hunt board and Welsh side chairs with pierced slats, circa 1810, complete the setting.*

HURRICANE HALL

In the lush Bluegrass country of Kentucky, back when that indomitable frontiersman Daniel Boone still wandered the region and Kentucky itself had just been carved from the edges of Virginia to become its own state, a large, simple, square, brick house was built by farmer David Laughed for his family near Lexington, county seat of Fayette County.

The house was whimsically dubbed "Hurricane Hall" — not for reasons of pretense or self-importance, but with a tongue-in-cheek touch of laconic Kentuckian humor. It was a place after all, its owner once exclaimed, where his numerous relatives came roaring up "like hurricanes" for extended visits. Halls have been named for less compelling reasons.

Still pleasant, easy and unself-conscious, the house is now the residence of a hospitable family in the horse-breeding business, and the old structure is as resolute and staunch of spirit as it was almost 200 years ago. Hurricane Hall is admired by visitors for its special sense of welcome and was singled out by architectural historian Clay Lancaster as "the most engaging residence in Fayette County."

Lexington, Kentucky, named, according to legend, in honor of Lexington, Massachusetts, the scene of one of the first battles of the Revolutionary War, was itself a city of some achievement and renown when Kentucky won its statehood. Considered the top-ranking inland cultural center north of New Orleans and west of the Alleghenies, it was often compared with Philadelphia and other port cities for enterprise and refinement.

For its part, Fayette County, the smallest of the three counties that originally comprised the 15th state of the Union, had been the focus of streams of immigration. Land grants following both the American Revolution and the French and Indian War had brought waves of settlers to the fertile valley, and the 280-square-mile county was to grow prodigiously during the 80 years between the Revolution and the Civil War.

Although there were no professional architects among the early citizens of Fayette, there were many nameless but skilled craftsmen. In their work with roughhewn logs, limestone and later brick, they followed their own instincts in using the materials available, employing techniques appropriate to the implements at hand. Combining their own concepts of simplicity and originality, Fayette County's craftsmen/builders brought forth architecture of a freshness and appeal that has not dimmed with time.

Hurricane Hall was built before 1800 on a 2,000-acre farm located on the upper part of the Georgetown Pike. It was a two-and-a-half-story brick structure, with high ceilings, lighted with four bay windows across the front and three across the back. The windows were 24-paned downstairs and 15-paned upstairs, a design brought to Kentucky from Virginia involving a subtle change of windowpane dimension.

The first floor consisted of a dining room, a parlor with presses flanking the chimney front, and a 15-foot-wide stair-hall which originally had a fireplace and was used as the main family living room. The staircase leading to the second floor continued on to a garret area believed to have been the accommodations for the house servants. The bed-chambers were located on the second floor. In the bedroom above the parlor, presses that adjoined the fireplace were adorned with pilasters framing paneled doors that opened to reveal a series of storage drawers, including a pull-out writing shelf.

In 1803, Roger Quarles bought the home from the Laughed family. He added a one-and-a-half-story stepped-down wing and connected the original detached kitchen pavilion to the main building. A new front porch encompassed by benches was built. Chamfered posts support the roof. In 1817, to commemorate the wedding of his daughter Sarah Jane to her cousin William Z. Thompson, Quarles had the hall and parlor hung with French scenic wallpaper. This decorative touch represented an extraordinary luxury for a frontier house because in many areas of Kentucky, householders were still struggling for survival, defending their homes from periodic attacks by marauding Indians. Another wing was added in the 1840's. It was also one-and-a-half-stories but was again stepped down from the 1803 addition and so attached that its two upstairs rooms could be lighted by windows at both gable ends.

At his death in 1856, Quarles willed the house to his grandson Patrick Henry Thompson who married Julia M. Farnsworth. As their family grew, the young couple decided to add another wing; it could be entered only from a rear gallery. The Thompsons eventually had nine children, and a school house was built which Mr. Thompson maintained for 35 years. During this time Hurricane Hall continued to live up to its name thanks to their boisterous activity.

The home remained in the Quarles family until 1962 when Mr. and Mrs. Stanley D. Petter, Jr., purchased it and began the task of renovation and restoration. Of the many dependencies that once stood to the west of the residence, a schoolhouse and a large smokehouse retain in part their original outlines, and traces of the foundations for the slave cabins beyond can be found.

The Petters have filled the house with treasured Kentucky pieces, books and paintings from both their families. Their successful Thoroughbred horse operation, Hurricane Stud, brings in countless friends and visitors; once again the old house is filled with people, and the tradition of friendliness and vibrant charm that Hurricane Hall has inspired through the years remains unchanged.

FACING PAGE. *Hurricane Hall is found deep in the heart of Kentucky's renowned Bluegrass region. Built when hostile Indians roamed the countryside, the house stands unrelenting, a notable example of antebellum architecture.*
ABOVE. *The 15-foot-wide entrance hall of Hurricane Hall originally had a fireplace and served as the main living space for the family. Today it displays a collection of English and Irish antiques.*
LEFT. *The living room was added to the house around 1805. The portrait above the mantel is of John Randolph, a man described by Thomas Jefferson as "unrivalled as the leader of the House" of Representatives. Edward Troye's painting above the antique desk from Western Kentucky is entitled* Heads or Tails.

PRECEDING PAGE. *The parlor, part of the oldest section of the house, features a paneled chimney breast with fine gougework, considered rare in this area of Kentucky. The portrait is signed "Mrs. Mary L. Duncan, wife of John M. Duncan. Mr. Joseph Bush, Artist, New Orleans, La. 1853." Wallpaper, hung in 1817 to commemorate a family wedding, is* Paysages d'Italie.

ABOVE. *The dining room table, made for Mrs. Petter's collateral ancestor John Randolph, is considered the most important piece of furniture in the house.*

RIGHT. *The back chamber, which has twin canopied beds, features a built-in press adjoining the fireplace.*

FACING PAGE. *Hurricane Hall's oldest room is the kitchen, which stood detached until the early-1800's. The huge open fireplace is still used and enjoyed by the Petter family.*

HAMPTON

Hampton, a place of brilliant hospitality in Maryland history, has been a Baltimore showplace since its completion in 1790. The discovery of iron ore on the original property in 1760 brought considerable fortune to the Ridgely family who later built this elegant mansion and lived in it through six generations. For those 158 years, the continuity of the Ridgely name and line was carefully protected and was a commanding force behind the sustained stewardship of Hampton.

This historic site is now operated by the National Park Service. The agency's Historic Structure Report of 1980 states that at the time it was purchased by the Avalon Foundation and donated to the United States government in 1948, the mansion and its outlying buildings were a "superb and unaltered example of a great southern slave plantation," and the main house was described as "one of 71 outstanding examples of Georgian architecture still in existence in the United States."

Hampton's 60 acres include an overseer's house, slave quarters, stables, dairy, orangery and other dependencies. The existing estate looks much as it did almost 200 years ago.

The Ridgelys were early settlers in the Colonies, and Colonel Charles Ridgely was a third-generation Marylander when he purchased the original tract of 1500 acres called "Northampton" for 600 pounds sterling in 1745. Adjacent lands were soon acquired for the cultivation of tobacco, wheat and corn, but the discovery of iron ore on the plantation in 1760 altered the property's destiny dramatically. Additional acres were annexed for mining purposes, and Northampton Ironworks was founded in 1761. The same year that iron was discovered, Colonel Ridgely conveyed the Hampton acres to his eldest son, also named Charles. These were the lands upon which Hampton would eventually be constructed.

The younger Charles prospered with the Revolutionary War, and already wealthy through family land speculations, shipping and ironworks, he planned a home on the Hampton estate that would complement his worldly success. Baltimore architect Jehu Howell is credited with building most of Charles Ridgely's impressive house, but marked contrasts in style and design indicate that two architects may actually have been involved.

Hampton incorporates touches of both Georgian and Palladian design. Particularly notable for its graceful balance, the house consists of a three-story "great" house and symmetrical smaller-proportioned flankers on each side, connected to the great house by "hyphens," or lateral room-sized passageways. A large hall extends through the center of the main house from the portico on the north to a mirror-image portico and facade on the south. The stairwell, informal parlor and dining room are located on the east side of the hall, and beyond is the connecting pantry which leads to the east wing and kitchen area. To the west of the main hall is a formal drawing room and music room; an adjoining wing was used as the plantation offices.

On Hampton's second level, the corridor is reversed and runs from east to west, allowing space for two large bedchambers (also used as sitting rooms for social gatherings) above the north and south porticos. It is on this floor that the interior architectural design appears notably changed; here, the Georgian woodwork is quite elaborate, while the first floor woodwork is executed in the simpler Federal style. Another level on the third floor, located within the eaves of the great house, is divided into ten small rooms, and a circular stairway winding upward from the third floor hall leads to a large domed cupola gracefully crowning the mid-center roof line. At the time of its construction and for almost 75 years thereafter, Hampton was one of the largest residences in America.

Charles Ridgely and his wife, Rebecca, moved into the mansion in 1788, three years prior to its completion. When Charles died without issue in 1790, controlling interest in the family ironworks was left to Charles Ridgely Carnan, a nephew and the husband of Rebecca's younger sister Priscilla Dorsey. The only condition to this proviso was that he reverse his middle and last names. This request was ultimately achieved by an act of the Maryland state legislature, and the "new" Charles Carnan Ridgely was thereafter granted leave to alter his name. Under the terms of her husband's will, Rebecca Ridgely was given the choice of residing at Hampton or at other property nearby. Choosing to relocate to a smaller residence, the widow relinquished Hampton to her sister and brother-in-law.

Charles Carnan Ridgely, dubbed the "General," was Governor of Maryland from 1815 to 1818. A famous host, he and his wife Priscilla entertained often and elegantly at Hampton. The General also maintained one of the finest racing stables of the time, and under his direction Hampton plantation, worked mainly by freed slaves, was renowned for its efficiency and productivity. The new owners also devoted much attention to the creation of formal gardens. Considered the largest earth-moving project of the 18th century, four terrace levels were carved out below the bowling green on the south side of the house. The top three terraces were divided into two parterres each, the bottom terrace being reserved for a kitchen garden. The overall design was taken from drawings submitted by artist William Birch and is thought to have been laid out by nurseryman William Booth.

John Ridgely and his wife Eliza, a celebrated beauty and heiress, inherited Hampton at the General's death in 1829. They were both well-educated, cultured and enjoyed extensive travel in Europe, where many new furnishings were selected and brought home to Hampton. Influenced perhaps by these trips abroad, Eliza decided to restructure the gardens. Guided by the principles of A.J. Downing, considered the father of American landscape architecture, the parterres were rearranged, and numerous exotic specimen trees, flowers and other plantings were added to the grounds. Unfortunately, John's many public and private interests did not include a talent for business, and over the next three decades the Northampton Ironworks was allowed to decline and ceased operation altogether by 1850.

At John Ridgely's death in 1867, his son Charles inherited Hampton. In turn, Charles' son John became master of the estate in 1872; he married Helen Stewart in 1873, and it was their son, the last John Ridgely to reside at Hampton, who sold the property to the Avalon Foundation in 1948.

Now a National Historic Site, Hampton presides authoritatively, a reminder of the grand achievements of one of the state's most venerable families.

FACING PAGE. *Hampton, a house enhanced with magnificent architectural details, was built for the Charles Ridgely family in 1790. Based on a plan of grand mid-18th century Maryland houses, it has a large central structure with wings attached by hyphens.*

ABOVE. *The dome of the house is reached from the third floor by climbing a staircase designed to conform to the twisting octagonal shape of the cupola.*

LEFT. *Above the south doorway of the great hall, the Ridgely arms are executed in colored glass, replacing the original clear glass. This is the only major change, with the exception of utilitarian additions, since the house was built.*

ABOVE. *Antique furniture in the sitting room includes a Chippendale wing chair and mahogany spinet made in Baltimore, 1830, by Joseph Hiskey. Portrait above the spinet is of Queen Mary II, wife of William of Orange.*

RIGHT. *Black and gold painted furniture in the drawing room was made by John Findley of Baltimore in the late 1820's. The gaming table, original to the house, is constructed of papier mâché with a checker-chess board top. A portrait of Nicholas Greenberry Ridgely hangs above the fireplace.*

FACING PAGE. *Broken arch pediments and a dentil carved cornice distinguish the dining room. The Sheraton sideboard, circa 1800, holds a large Chinese export porcelain punch bowl and round platter by Chaudron and Rascoe, Philadelphia, 1820. A Sheraton-style table is set with Sèvres porcelain.*

Elaborately detailed woodwork painted Wedgwood blue highlights the master bedroom. A tall secretary bearing a silver nameplate, engraved John England, 1723-1791, can be seen through the posts of a transitional Chippendale bed. A pair of Sheraton-style shield back chairs stand on either side of a pie crust tea table which is set with Staffordshire pink luster ware. The turkish rug was woven especially for Eliza Ridgely. It was found in the basement rolled up with tobacco leaves and has been restored to its original place in the house. The "wedding cake" chandelier was made prior to 1830; the protrait in the over-mantel is of Mrs. Charles Carnan Ridge-ly, artist unknown.

TOMBEE
PLANTATION

Probably no dwelling in America has experienced the human drama and natural calamities that have befallen Tombee Plantation on St. Helena Island, one of the beguilingly tranquil slips of land known as the Sea Islands. St. Helena, near Beaufort, South Carolina, was an early and important crucible of American history; it has played unwilling host to skirmishing colonial forces, marauding Spanish pirates and swashbuckling privateers since the early 16th century and has been the scene of bloody contention and fierce confrontations among Indians, blacks and whites for over 400 years.

Built on St. Helena about 1790 as home shelter and working base for one branch of the widespread Chaplin family, planters of indigo and cotton, Tombee's lands and its settlers were witness to sometimes peaceful, often ghastly, times — to Indian massacres, slavery and simmering rebellion, plagues and infestations, famines and hurricanes.

The old house has endured. It stands now rejuvenated facing out over the beautiful marshes of Station Creek.

ombee Plantation house, one of the few surviving structures of the 18th century remaining on St. Helena Island, was one of the smaller "big" houses built in the prosperous agrarian period between the Revolution and the Civil War. Here, on these fever-ridden marshlands, a handful of families carved out huge tracts of land, and employing the backbreaking labor of their many slaves, they built fortunes in cotton, indigo and other products. Contrary to popular myth, however, the "Low Country" planter's existence was a hard one. With their crops subject to devastation by caterpillars and worms, blight and floods, the owners of these vast plantations lived isolated and often beleaguered lives, separated by distance from each other's society and a boat's voyage from other land.

The Chaplin family was living on the island in the early 1700's when John Chaplin, Jr., established claim to property at Land's End on the southern tip of St. Helena. In 1715, the Yemassee Indians, together with their Creek allies, led an uprising that stretched from Cape Fear to St. Augustine. The three years of bitter fighting that ensued totally obliterated all early white settlements on St. Helena. In the end, however, the whites prevailed, making the region once again safe for colonization.

It is believed that Thomas B. Chaplin built Tombee about 1790 east of Land's End, facing out onto Station Creek. Ever-mindful of the great storms that frequently swept over the island, he built the house to last. He excavated a broad base five feet deep and filled it with tabby, a combination of sand, lime, oyster shells and water. Then, he built a raised, one-story-high tabby foundation on this base. It is this firm substructure that has given Tombee stability — a seeming imperviousness to weather, abuse, and neglect.

Similar in style to the fashionable residences of the coastal area, the home is a two-story, clapboard structure, with six square posts or pillars across its lower porch facade, which in turn support a matching six-pillar porch above. The house is built in the shape of a "T," with three rooms to each floor and is designed to provide maximum window exposure and ventilation. The windows themselves are nine panes over nine panes; there is one exterior chimney on each side of the house, and the floors are heart pine.

Thomas Benjamin Chaplin, a grandson of the original settler, was probably the man for whom this house was named. Born in 1822, he and his family made the plantation their home from 1845 until just after the Civil War. He was called Tom B., thus the designation of his residence as "Tombee."

Out of sight of neighbors, living with his immediate family and bonded slaves, it is no wonder that Chaplin became a compulsive diarist. His 780-page journal, now in the archives of the South Carolina Historical Society in Charleston, is a methodical and often plaintive record of the vicissitudes of a planter family's life.

The War between the States came to St. Helena; the Port Royal Experiment confiscated and divided Tombee and other plantations on the islands into units of land for freed slaves, and this policy continued through Reconstruction. The white masters left, and St. Helena became an island given over to former slaves. Tombee was occupied by black families for almost 100 years. Disillusioned and bitter, recalling happier times before his family lost their lands, Chaplin made one of his last journal entries in 1877. "Dear old home, how well I remember that very night, the bright warm fire that we went into, never to be again — never."

In 1971, Tombee was acquired by James A. Williams of Savannah, a zealous restoration expert knowledgeable in early architecture of coastal dwellings. No repairs had been done in the house for a century; it stood desolate among the live oaks, cedars and palmettos still facing the beautiful marshes of Station Creek. Although a hurricane in 1893 raised a flood tide of nine feet and a second flood tide rose to the floor joists of the main floor, the water had not completely erased the original blue-green paint on the ceiling moldings and on the stairs to the second floor. After a year's painstaking renovation, Williams obtained its listing in the National Register of Historic Places.

In 1977, Betsy and Alexander Yearley of Atlanta purchased Tombee from Williams. For convenience, a new one-story balustraded entry has been constructed at the rear and the original double-balustraded veranda still looks out over Station Creek.

The feather-graining on the paneling and overmantel and the wainscoting have been repaired. Two bathrooms and a kitchen have been added. The Yearleys have furnished Tombee with tasteful and appropriate early American and 18th-century English furniture.

Deeply appreciative of the history of St. Helena, the Yearleys have developed a loving empathy with old Tom B. Chaplin who they feel might have been writing to them in his day-to-day recountal. They search Tombee and its grounds for new evidence of its early life, and while no vestiges remain of the barn, kitchen, fowl house or smokehouse mentioned in his journal, they have found shards of fine china on the grounds. With a twinkle in her eye, Betsy Yearley concedes, "I'm tossing out a few shards of my own just to leave a trace of our happy use of this place too."

The Tombee house is strong and handsome again, and today a warm winter fire glows brightly within the same rooms recollected so yearningly in Tom Chaplin's lament for his "dear old home."

FACING PAGE. *Tombee Plantation, a two-story clapboard structure set on a high tabby foundation, is found on St. Helena Island near Beaufort, South Carolina. Built about 1790, the house was constructed in a T-shape with six main rooms, three upstairs and three downstairs.*

ABOVE. *Typical of the smaller plantation houses on Beaufort County's sea islands, the two-story house sits on a point overlooking an undisturbed marshland area.*

LEFT. *A view from the second story landing across the veranda to Station Creek and the Atlantic Ocean.*

FOLLOWING PAGE. *A copy of Thomas B. Chaplin's absorbing journal is kept on the ship surgeon's chest in front of the fireplace. The andirons and fender once belonged to Thomas Jefferson. The portrait is of Alexander Yearley I of Baltimore, great-great-great-grandfather of the owner. Armchair at the right was given to the Yearley family by Charles Carroll of Maryland, one of the signers of the Declaration of Independence. The rug is an Heriz.*

LEFT. *The mahogany pedestal table, circa 1840, is a family piece capable of seating twelve when fully extended. The chairs are thought to be Regency. The mantel displays classical motifs dominant during the Federal period.*

ABOVE. *An old French screen hangs above a Hepplewhite-style sideboard on which family silver is displayed.*

ABOVE. *An inviting upstairs bedroom has double exposure to insure adequate ventilation. The room features a plantation four-poster bed of cherry and a corner cupboard with broken pedimented top in which Chinese export porcelain is arranged.*

RIGHT. *An old pine table and captain's chairs from the home-owners' family rest comfortably on a multi-colored hooked rug in the kitchen. The china chest against the far wall is reputed to have been built at a Beaufort plantation by a local craftsman.*

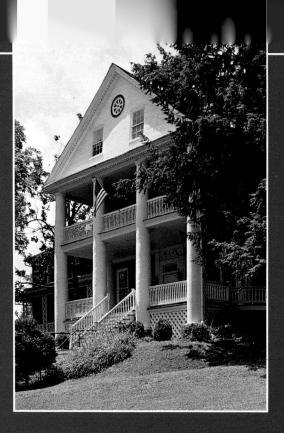

STUART HOUSE

Family tradition has it that Stuart House in Staunton, Virginia, was designed by Thomas Jefferson, who sketched its plan as a wedding present for his former law student and friend, Archibald Stuart. The residence was built in 1791 and bears the master's touch. Here and elsewhere in Virginia, the classical orders became a fundamental part of Southern architecture, a tradition honored to this day.

Seen from a distance, the formality of the soaring porch is softened by a welcoming Chinese Chippendale garden gate, capped by a gracefully stylized weathervane-finial. The mansion's verandas and balconies are marked by balustrades as fine and neat in appearance as starched white lace, and complementary crisp latticework skirts the foundation.

In 1975 when Justice George Cochran, a great-great-grandson of the first owner, inherited this historic manse, he and his wife were encouraged in their resolve to renovate by the discovery of a cache of historic documents, including letters to Archibald Stuart from colleagues and prominent political associates. Today, almost 200 years after its inception, Stuart House stands as a monument to the rich Southern heritage of a Virginia family.

Originally the home of Archibald Stuart, a Virginia lawyer and respected statesman of the 18th century, Stuart House was inherited by his great-great-grandson, Virginia State Supreme Court Justice George Moffett Cochran in 1975. Although well aware of their home's historic value, Justice and Mrs. Cochran were nevertheless surprised by their discovery of the astonishing treasure that lay beneath the eaves of the great house.

During the hot summer months of that same year, Dr. James Patrick, a Mary Baldwin College professor commissioned by the judge to catalog artifacts on the estate, came upon some 840 papers scattered amidst attic debris. Among them were letters from such notables as Daniel Webster, Sam Houston, John Marshall and President Millard Fillmore. One document, signed in 1800, contained a commission by then Virginia Governor James Monroe appointing Archibald Stuart a judge of the General Court of Virginia. Moreover, mixed in with a pile of refuse already tossed out the garret window, the Cochrans discovered law books which had once belonged to Jefferson, with marginal notes in his own handwriting.

More than 40 letters from Jefferson to his friend and confidant Archibald Stuart were already in the possession of the Virginia Historical Society in Richmond. This correspondence correlates the activities of these two influential men. During the same years that saw Jefferson author the Declaration of Independence and subsequently become the nation's third President, Stuart, one of the founders of the Phi Beta Kappa society, became a Revolutionary War officer, a presidential elector, judge and Virginia legislator.

With such historic impetus and the exciting trove of artifacts now lying unveiled at Stuart House, Mrs. Cochran, the former Lee Stuart of Elk Garden, Virginia, found she had a wealth of beautiful architectural details awaiting her reviving hand as well. All the handsome interior woodwork was intact, its rose and flame motif still clearly defined; interior pilasters with Ionic, Doric and Corinthian capitals and handcarved mantels with beautiful overmantels were all just as they had been originally; the "Heavenly Lord" hinges and brass locks on the doors still functioned, and most of the old windowpanes were unbroken.

A subsequent two-year renovation of Stuart House began. Drawing upon their home's richly detailed background, the Cochrans sought to maintain and preserve its architectural integrity while incorporating modern amenities. Some of the quaint reminders of 18th and 19th century life had already been sacrificed for the conveniences of the 20th century. Washstands with water pitchers and tin-footed tubs filled from cisterns had given way to running water and bathtubs, while lard-burning lamps with homemade wicks had been replaced with electricity and central heating. Further improvements and modernization of heating, plumbing and electrical facilities were necessary, as well as numerous structural repairs.

Despite these additions and modifications, the glories of the original features have been kept intact. Working from tracings of paint that remained beneath intervening layers, the Cochrans determined the 18th century wall colors, and the rooms and woodwork were repainted to match; paneling and wainscoting have been restored to their former beauty, and drapery treatments have been meticulously placed within the window frames so as not to obscure the carved surrounds.

Refurbishing Stuart House was a most rewarding task for Mrs. Cochran, who shares a distant ancestry with Archibald Stuart. Although the home's contents had been divided eleven times among successive descendants, some of the original period furnishings remained. The wardrobe and washstand belonging to the original mistress were still in her bedroom, as were her 1782 sampler and a leather basket of heavy keys to the larders. A grandfather clock remained majestically in place, and Archibald's signed Sheraton mahogany chair is again at home in the drawing room.

In a most fortunate coincidence, Mrs. Cochran's mother, Mrs. Harry Carter Stuart, had just disposed of the family estate in Elk Garden, Virginia. She offered the fine French furniture that Mrs. Cochran's great-uncle, Virginia Governor Henry Carter Stuart, had assembled to furnish the Governor's mansion during his tenure. Included in the precious collection was a Louis XV commode, heavily gilded with ormolu, which has a mate in the Schönbrunn Palace in Vienna. Mrs. Stuart also sent her own grandmother's elegant dining room set and a large portrait of Mrs. Cochran's great-great-uncle, Confederate General Jeb Stuart.

Now brightly refurbished and livable, its walls adorned with plaques from the Virginia Landmark Commission and the National Register of Historic Places, the revived old mansion recalls the Stuart family's vivid links with the past.

FACING PAGE. *Tradition has it that Stuart House, an 18th century plantation manor in Staunton, Virginia, was designed by Thomas Jefferson for his friend Archibald Stuart. Built in 1791, the house, carefully restored, has received plaques from the Virginia Landmarks Commission and the National Register of Historic Places. The unusual Chinese Chippendale gate at the entrance is noted in a separate register listing.*

ABOVE. *A view of the columned entrance to Stuart House from the porch that extends across the front of the 1841 addition.*

ABOVE. *Tapestry-covered French sofa and armchairs are prominently displayed in the spacious hallway. In a place of honor is the commanding portrait of Mrs. George M. Cochran's great-great-uncle, General James Ewell Brown Stuart, more familiarly known as Jeb Stuart. The rose and flame motif appears in the woodwork above both the drawing room and middle room doorways.*

FACING PAGE. *One of the many historic documents found in Stuart House is this commission appointing Archibald Stuart as a judge of the General Court of Virginia, signed by James Monroe.*

In the name of the Commonwealth
of Virginia:
To all to whom these presents shall come.
Know ye, that the General Assembly having by joint ballot
appointed Archibald Stuart a Judge of the General Court
the Governor of the said Commonwealth doth hereby Commission
him the said Archibald Stuart to have, hold, exercise and enjoy
that Office during good behaviour.

In Testimony whereof James Monroe Governor
of the said Commonwealth hath subscribed his name and
caused the seal of the said Commonwealth to be affixed
hereunto at Richmond this 25th day of January One
thousand eight hundred

Jas. Monroe

LEFT. *A portrait of Archibald Stuart, builder and first owner of Stuart House, is enclosed by the elaborate overmantel in which the rose and flame motif is carved. The Sheraton mahogany chair on the right is signed with Stuart's name.*

ABOVE: *A doorway leading from the middle room frames the drawing room in which a large oil portrait of Henry Peyton, an early Stuart ancestor, is displayed. The graceful sofa is late Empire.*

Above the Victorian fireplace in the dining room is a portrait of Justice George
M. Cochran, present owner of the
house. Chairs surrounding the table are
Chippendale and came from Mrs. Cochran's Elk Garden, Virginia, home as did
the china and crystal. An oil painting of
Mrs. Cochran's great-great-grandfather,
Dr. Alexander R. Preston, hangs above
the buffet. This room is located in the
1841 addition to the house.

ABOVE. *In the red bedroom, an elaborately carved four-poster bed owned by Governor Stuart is covered with an intricately crocheted spread. Chair rails break through the window jambs to form a continuous band with the sills.*
RIGHT. *The French furniture in this guest bedroom was purchased in Paris by Henry Carter Stuart for use in the Governor's Mansion in Richmond during his term of office, 1914-1918.*
FACING PAGE: *A handsome overmantel flanked by Ionic columns features a portrait of Alexander H. H. Stuart, Secretary of the Interior under President Millard Fillmore. The pair of high-backed arm chairs and the brass fireplace railing exhibiting a bamboo motif were inherited with the house.*

HAYS-KISER
HOUSE

*Located in Antioch, Tennessee, the Hays-Ki-
ser house stands without artifice as a straight-
forward example of late 18th century Federal
design. But the chronicle of its reclamation
from a nondescript architectural oddity to this
masterpiece of the genre is one that begins in
the mid-20th century.*

*It was the sight of an ambiguous advertise-
ment of sale — "175-year-old Victorian
house" — that first attracted the attention of
its present owners, Mr. and Mrs. John Kiser, in
1966. Since the age and purported style were
definitely contradictory, they decided to in-
vestigate. Their first view of the structure took
in the sight of a "funny-looking" old house.
To their delight, an unsuitable exterior addition of a two-story Victorian porch hid the
facade of a beautifully constructed residence.*

*Under the loving direction of John and
Jean Kiser, the residence has been restored to
its guileless integrity. Now thought to be the
oldest brick building standing in the county,
the Hays-Kiser house was listed in the National Register of Historic Places in 1974.*

There is both poignance and romance in the story of the Hays-Kiser house. The narrative begins in the late 18th century when three children, Tabitha, Nancy and Charles Hays, orphaned at an early age and reared by relatives and friends near New Bern on the North Carolina coast, married their childhood sweethearts — all from the same Blackman family — and followed each other west to establish new homes.

The first to leave was Tabitha. She had married Bennett Blackman, and together they made the more than 500-mile trek inland to settle territory then considered the western edge of North Carolina but which later became part of Tennessee. She was joined shortly thereafter by her sister Nancy and new brother-in-law John Blackman. When Charles Hays reached 18, he sold what remained of family property in eastern North Carolina, and preceding his fiancée Ann Blackman, followed the same arduous journey west through Cherokee-held lands, over the Appalachian Mountains, to what is now Antioch, Tennessee.

Young Hays quickly set about purchasing land from white settlers. Prudently deciding to stay on the good side of the Indians as well, he is said to have assured his welcome by paying his tribal neighbors six horses and ten bags of salt in return for all the land visible (2,500 acres) from his chosen hilltop homesite.

Charles began clearing land shortly before he and Ann were married in 1795, and using skilled workmen he had brought from North Carolina, he started constructing the house he had in mind for his bride. The structure is brick, a rarity in the region at a time when early buildings were chiefly frame and log, and is set on a cut limestone foundation with bricks laid in a Flemish bond pattern.

Following a plan popular in England and used by many builders in America during the 17th and 18th centuries, the main entrance opens directly into the parlor, the larger of two downstairs rooms. The adjacent smaller front room connects to an ell which at one time led to a detached kitchen and dining area constructed some distance away from the main block. A stairway leads from the smaller room to the second floor, where the same arrangement is followed. Upstairs, the larger room — the most elaborate chamber in the house — was probably inspired by the second-floor drawing rooms commonly found on the Eastern seaboard. Some years later, a second-story chamber known as "the boys' room" was constructed above the downstairs ell. It offered growing young men privacy since it could only be entered from the gallery of a two-story porch that was added at the same time.

In 1870, the house and a portion of the acreage were bought by members of the Rieves family who were to live there until 1965. The Rieves demolished the separate kitchen dependency, and enlarged the ell to extend the full width of the house which provided a kitchen and dining room on the first floor and another bedroom on the second. In 1894, they constructed a two-story porch across the facade, and following the design dictates of the times, so altered the home's appearance that it was thereafter termed a "Victorian" house.

In 1966, when John Kiser first peered into the living room window and saw the fine Federal woodwork, he entered to discover the crowning glory of the house: the magnificent poplar-paneled fireplace wall in the second-story "great" room, with its painted graining still in pristine condition. It was exactly as young Charles Hays had designed it for his bride.

After the Kisers acquired the house, they quickly ascertained that the original staircase had been removed; they were able to reconstruct another by using the outlines of the old stairwell balusters and handrails remaining under layers of wallpaper. Additionally, the original nine-over-nine windowpanes had been exchanged for Victorian era two-over-two panes, and the lovely old shutters were gone, as were most of the wrought-iron latches that held them in place. Fortunately, local craftsmen were able to replace and duplicate these items. The original colors of the interior woodwork were determined and matched, and the beauty of the exterior brickwork, hidden for years under a coat of red paint, was carefully restored.

Unfortunately, despite earnest efforts by the Kisers, none of Charles and Ann Hays' original furnishings have been found. Still, the new owners have thoughtfully and suitably decorated their charming residence with pieces dating from 1795 to 1854, the years Charles Hays and his family lived in the house. A copy of a large oil portrait of little Maria Louise Hays at 4, a granddaughter of Charles and Ann, hangs to the left of the front door . . . a sweet-remembered presence of the brave and proud lineage of the Hays-Kiser house.

FACING PAGE. *The Hays-Kiser house in Antioch, Davidson County, Tennessee, was built in 1795 by Charles Hays. Located about ten miles south of Nashville, the simple Federal structure is believed to be the oldest brick house still standing in that county.*

ABOVE. *The stairway leads from the front hall to the second floor where the hall and parlor floor plan is repeated. 19th century Oriental vases and a Meissen figurine, "Europa," decorate the beautifully carved mantel. On the far wall, a portrait of Sir Francis Hawkins, attributed to Henry Raeburn, hangs above a Queen Anne table of Yorkshire oak, circa 1750. The blue and white Meissen platter on the table is late 18th century. Oak chairs are Charles II style.*

PRECEDING PAGES. *The larger of the two rooms that make up the first floor of the main block of the house is the living room. Woodwork here and throughout the house is native poplar. Painting above the mantel is American 19th century, entitled* Winter Landscape, *attributed to Jasper Cropsey, 1823-1900. The sofa is a Philadelphia piece, circa 1825, and the lamp table, American Hepplewhite. Both the secretary and sewing basket are English Sheraton. Swan-backed open arm chair is from East Tennessee. The Oriental rug is Isfahan.*

ABOVE. *The dining room painting above the New York sideboard, circa 1825, is an imaginary landscape based on* A Midsummer Night's Dream, *and has a Maury County provenance.*

RIGHT. *Soft, gray painted woodwork and dark green mantel are colors original to the dining room. Handsome Rose Medallion porcelain graces the drop leaf table, which stands on an antique ingrain carpet, circa 1848. Side chairs are Empire, circa 1845, and childs chair, English, circa 1850. The clock is by Simon Willard.*

The most elaborate chamber in the house is the upstairs drawing room, now the master bedroom. Magnificent poplar paneled wall with its painted graining has never been altered and remains in impeccable condition. The overmantel painting, Scene from the Odyssey, is the work of 17th century French classical landscape painter, Jacques d'Artois, (1613-1684); the garniture is Ming Dynasty. Writing arm-Windsor is an early 19th century Tennessee piece and the lithographs in period frames are of Henry Clay and James K. Polk, distinguished Southerners.

HOPE
PLANTATION

Sojourners in quest of stately mansions must come upon Hope Plantation with surprise and delight. Set down amidst the flat fields of eastern North Carolina in the small town of Windsor, it is as festive as a wedding cake.

Sun-touched with the pale yellow of a fading jonquil, Hope's symmetrical proportions are beguilingly softened by fluttering touches of fresh white trim, an entrance of ascending steps with a crisp balustrade of Chinese Chippendale design, a two-story portico trimmed with the same ruching of Chippendale banisters and a white-framed square window in its peaked roof. The crowning touch is a widow's walk, also white, extending across the crest of the structure.

This is romantic Hope Plantation, a manor house built in the last decade of the 18th century for a young bride, the former Miss Hannah Turner, by her husband, David Stone, a brilliant and ambitious young man who was destined to become an important figure in North Carolina history.

The lands that comprised the original Hope Tract were acquired from the Lords Proprietors of the Carolina Colony in 1723 by members of the Hobson family and christened "Hope" in memory of the village they left far behind in Derbyshire, England. Inherited by Elizabeth Williamson Hobson at the death of her first husband, Francis, the property passed as a part of her marital estate to her second husband, Zedekiah Stone.

In 1793, Zedekiah deeded the Hope Tract's 1,051 acres to his and Elizabeth's son, David, as a wedding gift. This self-reliant young man of 23 was soon to marry Hannah Turner, daughter of a neighboring Bertie County planter, and after receiving the land from his father, he began construction of their new home. Although David Stone was apparently unaided by any professional architectural guidance, he had, close at hand, impressive examples of Georgian Colonial, including the distinguished Miles Brewton house in Charleston. He was also well-acquainted with the growing popularity of Jeffersonian classicism with its Palladian touches and had access to Abraham Swan's *The British Architect*, a well-read casebook of the times.

The house young Stone conceived is three-storied, with a pedimented central pavilion and hipped roof. A brick foundation is sufficiently high to allow the basement to be completely above the ground, and it contains a winter kitchen, several large storage rooms and a private back service stair leading to the top story of the house with exits on each floor.

A wide main hall runs through the center of the residence from front door to back, dividing the first floor in half; a grand dining room and a smaller family dining room are on one side, while two bedrooms are on the other. This Georgian-influenced "double house" plan provides all rooms with cross-ventilation from two outside exposures, as well as a cooling draft from the central hall, an excellent and practical arrangement for a warm climate. Unlike the stunning staircases in vogue at the time, Stone constructed a main stair encased between sealed walls ascending at the left side of the hall. Also indicative of this period are the large 16 x 20-inch windowpanes and the relatively small dimensions of the bedrooms when compared with the other rooms.

The most interesting and attractive spaces in the house are located on the second level — and perhaps no room at Hope Plantation reveals more about the original master of the house than the large, second-floor library set aside for his 1,400-volume collection. Housed in floor-to-ceiling cases covering two walls, the shelves are filled with books that touch on almost every academic discipline. The beautifully proportioned adjacent drawing room, with an Adam-style mantel and a handsome modillion cornice, opens onto the front upper level portico.

During and after construction of the mansion, David Stone continued to be active politically. His amazing career had begun at the precocious age of 14 when he was admitted to Princeton University. Four years later, he graduated at the top of his class, and at 19, he was a delegate to the North Carolina Constitutional Convention of 1789. He served as a member of the House of Commons of the North Carolina General Assembly for seven terms, two terms in the United States Senate and two terms as Governor of North Carolina.

After the death of Hannah, Stone married Sarah Dashiell of Washington, D.C. When he died in 1818 at the relatively young age of 48, he was one of the wealthiest men in North Carolina, having increased his holdings from just over 1,000 acres to nearly 8,000 acres and 138 slaves.

In the years that followed, Hope Plantation failed to prosper and by 1966, when Historic Hope Foundation, Inc. — a group of North Carolina preservationists — acquired the mansion and 18 acres of surrounding land, the property stood forlorn and dilapidated. The foundation was crumbling, windows and shutters were awry and most of the balustrade had been torn away.

Under the chairmanship of John E. Tyler, restoration was undertaken. Fortunately much of Hope's original interior woodwork and other architectural features were still intact. Remnants of many important details served as patterns for reconstruction: the remaining chimney served as a model for the other three; one fireplace and its beautiful mantel still survived to be copied, and an original window sash found in the basement helped form the others. The railing on the roof was gone, but with the Chinese Chippendale balcony railings of the front portico providing an example, replacements that were subsequently fashioned fit exactly in the openings from which the original structural members had fallen away.

Now authentically furnished with an excellent collection of period furnishings based on Stone's estate inventory, including some fine regional furniture, Hope Plantation is open to the public as a house museum.

FACING PAGE. *Hope Plantation was built during the late Colonial period in the early 1800's for Governor David Stone. Located near Windsor, North Carolina, it is an outstanding example of Georgian-Palladian architecture, a style characterized by pure symmetry, a pedimented central pavilion and hipped roof. It is listed in the National Register of Historic Places.*

ABOVE. *Front and back doors open into a spacious central hall, a recurring feature in Southern architecture. Chairs along the walls are part of the "2 10/12 dozen gray painted Windsor chairs," with red cushions referred to in Governor Stone's inventory. The small Pembroke table is original to the house, and the tall clock was made by Aaron Willard.*

FACING PAGE: *Prominent in the family parlor and informal dining room is an American bull's eye mirror. A Chowan County painted pine cupboard displays a collection of blue and white Canton china. A Chippendale chair in the French manner, circa 1760, stands before an embroidery frame on which a "Peacock's Eye" pattern is being worked, and an antique baby walker with bone rollers rests on an ingrain carpet.*

ABOVE. *An unusual three-piece Hepplewhite mahogany banquet table, circa 1795, is set with Bristol blue crystal and pearlware embellished with a chinoiserie design. A Chippendale-style silver plate tea caddy with wooden finial rests on the mantel beneath a portrait of Governor Stone. A Regency mirror hangs above the Hepplewhite-style sideboard attributed to Nehemiah Adams of Salem, Massachusetts.*

LEFT. *A handsome and unusual corner cabinet with bone inlay holds a collection of pearlware, creamware and Bristol blue crystal. Attributed to a cabinetmaker from the Roanoke River Valley, circa 1790-1800, it is one of the most important pieces in the collection.*

ABOVE. *The most interesting room at Hope Plantation is Governor Stone's library. Here two walls of floor-to-ceiling bookcases hold a portion of the 1400-volume collection covering a broad range of subjects. These books, reassembled from a list of contents made at the time of Stone's death, are available to qualified researchers.*

RIGHT: *The Chippendale desk with reverse serpentine front, circa 1760, was brought from New England by Governor Stone's father. A Queen Anne tripod table holding a backgammon board stands on a four-strip List carpet in tones of blue and brown. Country Chippendale-style chairs designed with a heart motif are from the Tidewater area of Virginia. Maps and surveys of the Carolina territory and the globes are further indications of the Governor's inquisitive nature.*

FACING PAGE. *The mahogany Hepplewhite-style bed and secretary in Governor Stone's bedroom are from the Federal period. A rare homespun white-on-white spread with fine drawn work was made by a local girl for her hope chest in the 18th century.*
ABOVE: *The second floor drawing room is highlighted by an Adam-style mantel with fireplace facings and hearth of Italian marble. Andirons are signed "R. Wittingham, N. York." The richly carved and gilded mirror is English. Both the violin and pianoforte were listed in the Governor's original inventory.*
LEFT. *A Low Country South Carolina "rice bed" features carved rice fronds, acanthus leaves and reeding.*
FOLLOWING PAGES. *The winter kitchen in the high basement is typical of those found in plantation houses in the 18th century. Peppers and herbs, hung to dry from the ceiling beams, were used in cooking and medicines. Antique chairs with split-oak seats and a wide-board pine table are characteristic of the time.*

97

LIVE OAK

The sun-dappled fanfare of ancient live oaks extends a sheltering welcome over the avenue which leads to an alluring old plantation house named in their honor: Live Oak in Feliciana Parish, Louisiana.

Live Oak was built sometime in the turbulent years of change between 1800 and 1816, before the area became the 18th state of the Union. It is an early and important example of an Anglo-American plantation house in the days when families focused their entire lives — shelter, growth, pain, sorrow, pleasure, celebration — on their own hearthsides. Their homes bespoke their response to challenge, their pride of possession and, tacitly, their realization of great fortunes within reach of those daring enough to seize them.

Located near the center of 115 acres and at some distance from Little Bayou Sara, Live Oak is unpretentious, enchantingly appealing and secure. Unlike its more opulent and lavish Louisiana plantation-house neighbors, it has a subtly suggested primness, an enduring discipline reminiscent of the restraint of the smaller "great" houses built on the Eastern seaboard in the early 1800's.

Live Oak is located on lands that were part of a Spanish concession of 1,000 acres granted to Alexander Ross in 1796. By 1802 the tract was in possession of Elijah Adams and his brother-in-law, William Cobb. They divided the property equally, and Adams' five hundred acres became the supporting land for Live Oak plantation. The exact year of construction is not known, but built sometime between 1800 and 1816, it was one of the earliest homes in the area. Its architecture not only relates to Anglo-American building ideas brought by settlers from the Eastern coastal states and from the Natchez area, but also to the French and Spanish influences already prevalent in the area.

The house is two-storied, with gabled ends, and has heavy plastered brick columns (a Spanish echo) which support upper galleries. It is made entirely of whitewashed brick, a material usually used only for the basement story. Exterior staircases — typical Louisiana-French elements — lead to the upper story, front and back; fireplaces and chimneys are placed on the end walls in the Anglo-American mode.

Live Oak has the practical floor plan which the French used frequently in the new "Land of Louis": upper and lower floors consisting of two rooms side by side, front and back, with well-ventilated chambers opening directly onto outside galleries and no space lost to interior foyers or halls. Front hall entrance doors are paneled and open outward like shutters, with rectangular transoms divided into five lights above. In addition, each front room has a large double-hung window with louvered shutters opening to the gallery and narrower double-hung windows flanking the fireplace on the end wall. Elegant mantels in each of the four front rooms, two on each floor, are of the Federal style, elaborately detailed with pilasters, moldings, reedings and gouge work. In the left front room, an interesting enclosed "sneak" stairway, 18 inches in width, is concealed behind a series of three paneled doors adjacent to the fireplace. The stairwell leads to the bedroom above, and the landing at the second floor is enclosed by a delicate railing with square newels, slender balusters and a molded handrail.

The builder of this house, Elijah Adams, was an officer in the 10th and 20th Consolidated Regiments of Concordia and Feliciana Parishes. Captain Adams was to fight in the Battle of New Orleans; the campaign so wrecked his health that he died one year later in 1816. His plantation was purchased by his daughter Charlotte and her husband Amos Webb. About the same time, an inventory of one Peter Murray, a carpenter, revealed that Murray was owed a sum of money for work done at Live Oak. Thus Murray may have executed the fine interior woodwork and per-

haps supervised construction of the house itself.

In 1824, Live Oak was acquired by Bennett Barrow, a member of one of the wealthiest and most prominent families in the state. Live Oak remained in their descendants' possession for more than a century. One hundred and four years later, in 1928, the plantation was purchased by Mr. and Mrs. William LeSassier. One of the downstairs rooms was used as a post office, and the upstairs was converted to a school for neighborhood children.

Live Oak, with its 115 surrounding acres, is now the property of Bert and Sue Turner of Baton Rouge. When they acquired the old house, it was severely dilapidated — all that remained of the plantings were one azalea and a few old crape myrtles and the magnificent live oaks.

Under the direction of New Orleans architect Samuel Wilson, Jr., of the firm Koch and Wilson, the Turners have undertaken a careful and loving renovation to return Live Oak to its original state. Repair to the brickwork was extensive. Cypress, pine and ash flooring on the ground level was taken up, numbered and stored. Digging down to the foundation, they found that the original floor joists had been timbers reused from barges which had floated on the Mississippi. The framing and all interior woodwork was found to be blue poplar. A few pieces of the original handwrought hardware were still existent and served as models for duplication where replacements were needed.

Originally there had been a detached kitchen, but the Turners decided to adapt the larger of two ground floor rear rooms for a new kitchen. The smaller rear room, with its corner fireplace, is now a study. Upstairs, two small bedrooms at the back were converted to baths, leaving the old wooden floors and corner fireplaces intact. The attic level, unfinished until the Turners' acquisition, has now become a recreation and sleeping area, with a new pale poplar wood floor blending with old ceiling beams.

Under the direction of John Geiser III, a New Orleans specialist, plaster was stripped from the walls throughout the house, and layers of paint were scraped from the doors and woodwork. Although there was evidence of marblizing on much of the woodwork and in all of the second-story rooms between the chair rails and base molds, the Turners decided to use white walls everywhere; one *faux bois* door was preserved.

The gardens have now been reestablished. All of the blooming plants are white — azaleas, roses, calla lilies and daffodils. Brick walls for the formal garden and a rear brick terrace have been added. The handsomely furnished newly restored Live Oak has been placed on the National Register of Historic Places and is recorded by the Historic American Buildings Survey. It is open to pilgrimages and groups by appointment.

LEFT. *Located in Louisiana's West Feliciana Parish, Live Oak Plantation stands at the end of a wide avenue of live oaks. The setting remains much as it was in the early 1800's. The 1808 plantation house reflects the early Anglo-American influence of settlers from the Natchez area and the Eastern seaboard.*

ABOVE. *An antique tin-lined cellaret is placed under the window in one corner of the parlor. An English Chippendale chair stands beside a tripod birdcage tilt-top tea table displaying an English Argand lamp, circa 1830. A Catesby print,* Kingfisher, *is placed between the windows.*

The parlor is decorated with white walls and blue trim. Bare windows, the only ones in West Feliciana Parish with splayed jambs, bring in the verdant outdoors. An English Queen Anne burled walnut accordian action card table stands in front of the sofa. An Audubon first print by Lazar, Great American Cock Male, hangs above a French Louis XV buffet, circa 1850, which is flanked by English mahogany chairs. The Martha Washington chair is early 19th century. The bronze and ormolu chandelier is French, circa 1830.

ABOVE. *French doors open to the lower gallery and the impressive avenue of live oaks beyond. A botanical print showing native Louisiana plants hangs above an American dropleaf table exhibiting two Argand lamps. The rug is an antique Serapi.*

RIGHT. *A 19th century cypress table from Myrtle Grove Sugar Refinery, once owned by Mrs. Turner's family, is set for brunch in the dining room, the second principal room on the ground floor. Dogwood, iris, winter wheat and vines are arranged in an old iron urn serving as a centerpiece. The china is Spode. A tôle, bronze and ormolu chandelier, circa 1830, hangs above. Handmade fruitwood chairs are Spanish. French tôle chestnut urns, circa 1835, adorn the mantel.*

LEFT. *A 19th century cypress high-post bed and a 19th century cypress low buffet from the Ursuline Convent in New Orleans are found in the guest bedroom. The rush-bottom chair and the prie-Dieu beside the bed are French.*

ABOVE. *A four-board American chest, featuring original green paint in a* faux bois *finish, stands at the foot of the 19th century carved South Carolina tester bed in the master bedroom. The "Friendship" quilt once belonged to Mrs. Turner's grandmother. An antique tôle hatbox is used as a table beside the 18th century Pennsylvania daybed. The rug is an antique Mowri.*

RICHARDSON-OWENS-THOMAS HOUSE

Located in Savannah, Georgia, a city which evolved from early days as a lusty seaport settlement to preeminence as a cultural center known for its charming and historic residences, the Richardson-Owens-Thomas house on Oglethorpe Square is recognized as perhaps the city's most important architectural expression arising from the early 1800's.

It was created by the young British architect, William Jay, who brought with him from Bath, England, images of design and style that were clearly more than just suitable dwellings for the very rich. The house was a new architectural point of view for the Port of Savannah, which was beginning to enjoy a time of immense prosperity.

The mansion's reserve and balance declared from the beginning that here was a structure which must prevail. A landmark when it was completed in 1819, the house is a monument to the efforts of preservationists.

As one of history's caprices, a discrepancy of dates in the provenance of the Richardson-Owens-Thomas house stands out. William Jay, its architect, did not arrive in Savannah until a year after the house was well under way. Moreover, when it was completed in 1819, an inscription incised on the masonry foundation by its builder, local contractor John Retan, conveyed only this information: "Began house A.D. 1816—finished June A.D. 1819—J. Retan." Nevertheless, commissioned by Richard Richardson, a Savannah banker and merchant, the mansion's Classic Revival architecture is with good reason ascribed to the talents of Jay, who had become acquainted with Richardson through a family connection.

It is thought that the twenty-one-year-old architect designed the house prior to leaving England and sent the preliminary plans ahead of his arrival. Although proof of this theory has not yet been found, it is certain that Jay was on hand to bring the house to completion, and he is universally credited with its success. Twenty-three years later in 1842, James Silk Buckingham, a well-known British traveler and author, enthusiastically reported: "In Savannah there are a few mansions built by an English architect, Mr. Jay, son of the celebrated divine of that name at Bath—which are of beautiful architecture, of sumptuous interior and combine as much of elegance and luxury as are to be found in any private dwelling in the country."

Richard Richardson, the first master of this particular sumptuous abode, was one of the new class of merchant magnates whose great wealth could be attributed to the burgeoning American economy following the War of 1812. The port town of Savannah was also enjoying unparalleled prosperity due to the cotton trade, and Richardson, a beneficiary of these boom times, could well afford to build his home in the latest and most fashionable manner. This was the period of the regency of George, Prince of Wales (1811-1820), and a new restrained but majestic style was emerging from England. The elite of Savannah, always more influenced by British and northern tastes than those of their own region, saw in the commanding new architecture what they hoped to reflect in their own destinies. Richardson's house became one of the first to mirror this Classical Revival mode which prevailed—along with King Cotton—for the next three decades.

In 1819, Petit de Villiers, a Savannah merchant, wrote to General Charles Cotesworth Pinckney, Pinckney Island, ". . . You would be astonished to see the number of handsome fire-proof dwelling houses that have been completed here since the last war and those that are now erecting.

There are several houses here that would be an ornament to any city." This was the same year that William Jay's magnificently designed dwelling for Richardson was nearing completion. Built of materials to better withstand fires such as those that had devastated large sections of Savannah in the years preceding Jay's arrival, the Regency mansion was constructed on one of the Trust lots laid out by Colonial Trustee James Oglethorpe in his 1733 plan for Savannah.

This large corner site in the oldest part of the city was a perfect location to profile the imposing two-story house. Now weathered to the antique lightstruck patina of a Renaissance villa, the austere main facade is softened by a double entrance with curving steps, iron balustrades and a columned front portico bowed slightly in welcome. The unique four-pillared "William Jay" balcony on its south, East President Street, face, which has been termed one of the most stunning and exceptionally lovely verandas in early-American architecture, is the same noble dais from which the Marquis de Lafayette spoke to the public in 1825 on his last visit to America. Adjacent to the house and balcony is a walled garden, a portion of which can be seen from the street.

Inside, still respecting classical orders, Jay introduced his own surprising melodic three-dimensional composition: concave ceilings; sculptured and intaglio moldings; and graceful wall niches indirectly illuminated from behind Greek Key filagreed glass and plaster screens.

Before he left Georgia in 1820 for Charleston, South Carolina, Jay was to design four or five additional houses and several other buildings, among them the new Savannah branch of the Bank of the United States for its president and his original client, Richard Richardson.

In 1822 after his wife's death, Richardson sold the mansion. It was used briefly as a boarding house until 1830 when George Welchman Owens purchased it. For the next 121 years it was the residence of the Owens family and their descendants. In 1951, Margaret Gray Thomas, Owens' granddaughter, willed the house to the Telfair Academy of Arts and Science to be used as a house museum.

Writing in her book *The Houses of the New World,* Fredericka Bremer summarized her impression of the coastal city she was describing in the year 1854: "There cannot be in the whole world a more beautiful city than Savannah. It is an assemblage of villas come together for company." Today, 130 years later, this statement still rings true, and the Richardson-Owens-Thomas house, the crowning "ornament" of this august gathering, continues to reign supreme.

FACING PAGE. *Often called "the finest Regency house in America," the Richardson- Owens-Thomas house, designed by English architect William Jay, set the standard for domestic architecture in Savannah, Georgia, in the 1800's. The balcony on the south side is cast iron painted to resemble stone. Plans calling for a matching balcony on this elevation were never completed. Today, fully restored, furnished and preserved as a house museum, it stands as a National Historic Landmark.*

ABOVE. *Busts of Lord Byron and Sir Walter Scott on consoles flank fluted columns with gilded capitals in the Greek Corinthian Order in the vestibule. Staircase balusters are of iron with a mahogany handrail inlaid with brass.*

Furniture in the reception room, including a sofa by Duncan Phyfe, is American, circa 1830. Highlights of the room are the ceiling, designed by William Jay in the manner of English neo-classicist, Sir John Soane, and mantelpiece attributed to English sculptor, Richard Westmacott, Jr. The portrait of Anne Jay Bolton by William Etty, R.A., is on indefinite loan from the New York State Historical Society.

The most unusual design feature of the dining room is the shallow niche, which provided indirect lighting rather than a window on the north wall. The marble-top Regency console on carved mahogany and ebony pedestal in the niche is original. Banquet table and chairs are American from Philadelphia. Pine floors painted alternately dark and light are original to the house.

ABOVE. *Furnishings in the second floor library/sitting room are 19th century American. The portrait above the mantel is of Robert Bolton, husband of Anne Jay Bolton, William Jay's sister, and is on indefinite loan from the New York State Historical Society.*

RIGHT. *An unusual bridge connecting the front and rear of the second floor, which gives the center of the house a feeling of spaciousness, was an adaption by Jay on designs by 18th century English architect, Sir John Soane, who was called the "master of surprises in internal space."*

FACING PAGE. *A second floor bedroom is furnished as it might have been when the French patriot, the Marquis de Lafayette, visited the house in March 1825. The bed is Regency, circa 1800; the rug, Turkish Oushak. The New York State Regency table is surrounded by Sheraton fancy chairs.*

ARLINGTON

Arlington, a classically pillared Old South residence, is located three miles west of the downtown heart of Birmingham, Alabama. The mansion is the city's only surviving Greek Revival antebellum home and predates the establishment of Birmingham itself by almost 30 years.

First known as "The Grove," then "Mudd House," Arlington takes its present name from the property on which it stands . . . "Arlington Survey," a subdivision developed around it in 1886 by the third owner, Franklin H. Whitney. The city of Birmingham bought the house in 1953, and the historical showplace is open to the public year around.

Dogwood and cherry trees line the walkway leading to the house. On the grounds, a romantic walkway formed by carefully trimmed hedges leads to a summerhouse, which is maintained for weddings and other social gatherings.

Arlington is located in Elyton (a section of Birmingham, Alabama), the first permanent county seat of Jefferson County and a center of trade and culture for 50 years prior to the establishment of the great steel-producing city which grew up around it. In 1822, a year after Elyton's incorporation, the property on which Arlington stands was acquired by Stephen Hall, who constructed a home overlooking the small settlement. Hall's son Samuel inherited the property, and after his death in 1842, the house and 16 acres of land were sold at public auction for $600.

The purchaser was William S. Mudd, a lawyer who served several terms in the state legislature and for 25 years sat on the bench as a Circuit Court judge. Shortly after acquiring the property and 80 additional adjacent acres in 1842, Judge Mudd built a new home on the estate which reflected the Greek Revival style of architecture. Neither the exact date of construction nor the name of the architect is known. The Mudds called their spacious abode "The Grove" and reared nine children here, tucking them snugly into the four upstairs corner bedchambers.

During the Civil War, the Confederacy sought to exploit the mineral rich area in Jefferson County by helping build a railroad line from the military district to the Confederate military arsenal at Selma. As a consequence, "The Grove" had its own brief brush with the war in 1865. One month before the conflict's end, General James H. Wilson, who headed Union troops known as Wilson's Raiders, paused at the Mudd residence long enough to deploy contingents to destroy nearby Confederate industries, munition stores and the military school at the University of Alabama at Tuscaloosa. General Wilson dismissed the little town of Elyton as ". . . a poor, insignificant Southern village, surrounded by old field farms, most of which could have been bought for $5 an acre."

Wilson's contemptuous appraisal of the "old field farms" was soon proved premature. By 1871, the two rail lines which had been started by the Confederacy were extended to converge at a cornfield three miles east of Elyton. The crossing was named Birmingham, a community which immediately began its successful drive toward becoming one of the great industrial centers of the nation.

Henry F. Debardeleben, one of the developers of Alabama's rich iron and coal resources, bought "The Grove" and its surrounding acres after Judge Mudd's death in 1884. He did not occupy the house, however, and sold most of the estate to the railroad; two years later, he sold the house itself, along with 33 acres of remaining property, to Franklin H. Whitney, of Iowa. It was Whitney who divided the property into residential lots, naming the subdivision "Arlington Survey." In 1902, six years after Whitney's death, the house passed into the hands of Robert S. Munger, an inventor, manufacturer and philanthropist. The mansion was almost in ruins.

The Mungers first used Arlington as a summer retreat. They replaced the old detached kitchen with a separate building which served as kitchen, dining room and servants' quarters. They added plumbing, electricity and central heating, and eight years later, moved into their renovated residence permanently. They lived here for the next 14 years. Following the deaths of Munger and his wife in 1924, their daughter Ruby and her husband Alex Montgomery inherited the house and remaining six acres. The city of Birmingham bought the house from the Montgomery family in 1953 for $50,000.

The basic gracefully symmetrical design of Arlington has not been changed through the years. It is almost square, with a wide reception hall dividing the first floor . . . two parlors on one side, a music room and dining room on the other, with porches and balconies at front and back. The pattern is repeated on the second floor, with four bedrooms placed at each corner.

During the Mungers' occupation, the two downstairs parlors were converted to one large drawing room, and the ceiling heights of several other rooms were changed. The construction of Arlington, now revealed in a cutout of the music room wall, is noteworthy: plaster applied over wall lathing was strengthened with the addition of horsehair. The house rests on handhewn, heart pine timbers interlocked with mortice-and-tenon joints. To prevent termite damage and wet rot, the timbers were based on a foundation bed of stones. The original mid-19th century floor of wide heart pine planks has been replaced with 20th-century tongue-and-groove pine planks overlaid with narrow oak veneer.

In an amusing note, Arlington lore has it that Mr. Munger remodeled a small cantilevered front balcony into a strong full-width front porch because of concern for his wife's safety. It seems that her love of outdoors, together with her healthy proportions and imperfect balance motivated her husband to build a more substantial "perch."

The furnishings at Arlington are not original to the house nor to the families who occupied the mansion but are representative of the mid-19th century, with some earlier pieces. Wallpaper, carpets, draperies and paint colors have been chosen to complement the furnishings and capture the nostalgic charm of a mid-19th century Southern plantation home.

LEFT. *Beneath the Louis XV chandelier is a handsome Hepplewhite-style banquet table, circa 1800. The accompanying mahogany veneer sideboard is Sheraton-style, circa 1810. The chairs are English Regency, circa 1810.*

TOP. *The four poster maple bed in the corner bedroom was referred to as a "field bed," because it resembles an army officer's tent. It holds a double weave jacquard coverlet bearing the inscription, "Hannah Warburton wove in 1839." The washstand, mason ironstone pitcher and washbowl were standard pieces of bedroom furnishings in the 1900's. The bow back Windsor chair, circa 1850, was originally painted green and is signed "S.B." in yellow on the bottom of the seat.*

ABOVE. *Seen from the west side of the house is the summer house which was built about 1910. It is presently used for special occasions such as weddings and receptions.*

THE
GORDON-BANKS
HOUSE

The Gordon-Banks house was built in 1828 as a comfortable residence for a prospering plantation family by a young carpenter-architect. As the Civil War seized its last fierce grip on Georgia, the stately structure was commandeered briefly by Union General Francis Blair. For the next century, it endured a succession of owners and occupants, until, in 1968, when the house was 140 years old, it survived a 100-mile removal to the Piedmont area of Georgia. Now resettled amid azaleas and dogwoods on the crest of a knoll overlooking a small lake at Bankshaven, the Gordon-Banks house is one of the finest historic homes in the nation.

he Gordon-Banks house overlooks an immaculately preened vista on a summit of Bankshaven, an estate in Newnan, Georgia. It has been carefully restored and elegantly furnished by its owner, William Nathaniel Banks, a Georgia writer and art collector in conjunction with his mother, the late Mrs. William N. Banks, Sr. At the recommendation of the National Trust for Historic Preservation, Mrs. Banks and her son engaged architect Robert L. Raley to supervise moving the house from a site near Milledgeville to its present location. Landscaping of the estate, begun in the 1920's, was developed according to a plan by architect William C. Pauley. An acreage with great natural beauty of terrain, woods and water, it was nurtured devotedly by the late William N. Banks, Sr., father of the present owner.

The classical ornamentation and impeccable interior detail of the Gordon-Banks house are more remarkable since the structure was designed and built by a young carpenter-architect.

Daniel Pratt was 20 years old when, in 1819, he left his native New Hampshire, sailed south on the brigantine FAVORITE and, with $25 in his pocket, paused in the growing coastal city of Savannah to further his fortune.

A year later, Pratt moved on to Milledgeville, then the capital of Georgia and a thriving center of agriculture, where it is believed he found work with John Marlor, an architect from England, in practice there. It was soon evident that his time in Savannah had not been wasted. As a carpenter, he had observed the polished interiors by William Jay of Bath and London, the handsome Federal buildings of Adrian Boucher and Isaiah Davenport, all of whose influences were being felt in the developing seaport. He is also believed to have studied the design books of Asher Benjamin, especially *American Builder's Companion,* published in 1806.

For the next decade, using architectural skills derived from observation and reference, together with his own instinct for proportion and structure, Pratt worked in and around Milledgeville. At least eight residences in the region have been attributed to his hand.

The Gordon-Banks house, located in a hamlet called Haddock, Georgia, was undertaken for General John W. Gordon, cotton planter, state senator and brigadier general in the Georgia militia. Several years were spent completing the residence, its dependencies and elaborate gardens.

The anatomy of all Pratt's houses was similar. Their facades and proportions were appealingly classical, but in the main they were suited to the demands of clients and the considerations of cost. Even the floor plans of the houses were similar: wide central halls leading to curving staircases dividing the houses in half; two large front rooms; two smaller back rooms; a two-story portico supported by columns, with a second floor balcony.

But in the Gordon-Banks house his joy was in the ornamentation, detail that still delights discerning critics. A beautiful fanlight spans the double front door, its radiating design springing from a sunburst motif. A series of ovals and circles decorates the top chords. A more shallow fanlight spans the double doors of the second-floor balcony. Banisters, balusters, pilasters, the sweep and grand height of the curving stairs, niches on either side of the parlor fireplace, gilded cornices and plaster moldings, woodwork accented with rich colors, marbelized baseboards all bespeak Pratt's love of ornamentation.

After practicing his trade as an architect-builder for ten years, Pratt moved to Clinton, Georgia, where he assumed supervision of a cotton gin factory owned by Samuel Griswold, a neighbor. In 1833, he moved with his family and two Negroes to Alabama, taking the materials for 50 cotton gins. Five years later, he purchased a tract near Montgomery, naming it Prattville, and established one of the leading manufacturing concerns in the South.

In 1848, General Gordon sold his house to Thomas O. Bowen. The Bowen family lived in it through the Civil War. Bowen sold it in 1881 to James H. Blount of Macon. At his death, Blount left the house to his daughter, Mrs. Walter D. Lamar. As had her parents before her, Mrs. Lamar used it only for a weekend retreat.

In the 1940's, L.C. Lindsley, a teacher and historian, acquired the house. He repaired it and kept it lovingly until his death. Lindsley's daughter, Mrs. John James, sold the house in 1968 to the late Mrs. Banks. It had been only intermittently occupied for over 50 years.

The Gordon-Banks house, now a beloved private residence, fits at Bankshaven as majestically as if it had been there all of its 156 years.

FACING PAGE. *The fanlight over the equally proportioned front door is a fine example of architect Daniel Pratt's handling of over-scaled interior elements. The great expanse of glass emits light into the spacious central hall, which opens onto a broad portico and the manicured scene beyond.*

ABOVE. *Built for General John W. Gordon in 1828, the neoclassical Gordon-Banks house is framed by native dogwoods and azaleas.*

FACING PAGE. *Decorative details in the front parlor of the Gordon-Banks house include skillfully molded plaster details of classical flowers and leaves in the cornice. Gilded rosettes enrich upper corners of the window frames while gilded plaster leaves and stop-fluted pilasters frame the semicircular fanned niches. Above the original mantel with reeded and fluted columns is a classical French clock made by Jean André Lepaute, 1720-1789, and convex girandole mirror from the early 19th century. Notable in the room are a Philadelphia settee inscribed "Sam'l McIntire, 1805" and a sewing table, circle 1800, which stand on an Aubusson rug. The chandelier is French Empire.*

ABOVE. *The pianoforte in the front parlor was made by John Broadwood and Sons of London, circa 1810.*

LEFT. *The card table with winged caryatid support, circa 1815, attributed to cabinetmaker Charles Honoré Lannuier, is the piece that kindled William Banks' interest in collecting American furniture and the subsequent restoration of the then Gordon house.*

Standing on a fine 19th century French needlepoint rug, circa 1830, in the dining room are Federal lattice-back chairs from Massachusetts and an English pedestal table, circa 1825, set with Old Paris porcelain. The door and dado paneling are painted to imitate flame mahogany veneers with tiger-maple borders. Gilded plaster flowerets adorn the cornices of the door and window frames. The portrait of Mrs. William N. Banks, Sr., is by Charles Naegele.

ABOVE. *Three distinguished Empire pieces, a circular pedestal table and a pair of Greek Revival couches attributed to the Philadelphia cabinetmaker, Anthony Quervelle, are in the spacious upper stair hall, which was designed as a sitting room. The painting above the sofa is by Severin Roesen; the rug, Aubusson with an 18th century design. On the staircase, a carved and gilded scroll motif can be seen against the marbleized stair frame, the Vitruvian scroll around the upper stairwell is repeated in the parlor.*

RIGHT. *Over the mantel in the master bedroom is one of a number of fine American paintings at Bankshaven. The title of the work is* Gathering Wood for Winter, 1855, *by George Henry Durrie. The mahogany-and-maple tester bed is early 19th century.*

ABOVE. *A guest bedroom displays an early 19th century Louisiana bed that once belonged to a former governor of that state.*

LEFT. *Another guest bedroom holds a mahogany alcove bed with ormolu decoration in the French Empire style. The original bill of sale, dated "1813 March 13," documents it as by Duncan Phyfe, New York City. Carving on the lyre-back chairs, circa 1800, is characteristic of the New York cabinetwork of the period.*

FACING PAGE. *A broad arch separating the stairwell from the main entrance hall is highlighted by gilded plaster leaves. Pilasters fluted on two sides and paneled on a third support the arch. Baseboards are decorated with original marbleizing. The pier table is attributed to Charles Honoré Lannuier.*

ABOVE. *Above the large New York State bookcase in the study is a landscape painting by Albert Bierstadt. A worktable stamped by Rufus Pierce of Boston, Massachusetts, stands between a pair of Boston chairs on a Caucasian rug. Painting above the mantel is by Asher B. Durand.*

LEFT. *The Venetian pool pavilion was designed by Ella Mae Ellis League of Macon, Georgia.*

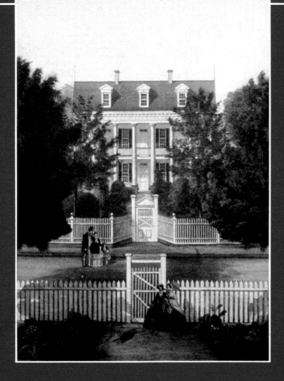

SHADOWS-ON-THE-TECHE

The hauntingly beautiful name "Shadows-on-the-Teche" evokes the lush and verdant Bayou Teche (pronounced Tesh) countryside that surrounds and sets the scene for this gracious town house in New Iberia, Louisiana. In its busy, useful years, it was simply called "Home Place" by the family of David Weeks, an adventurous man who built it in 1831 as the residential heart of his acreage for the cultivation of sugarcane, or "white gold" as it was known among the delta planters.

It was William Weeks Hall, the last private owner of the manor and a great-grandson of David Weeks, who began the restoration in 1922. He recognized that the appeal of the old residential monument was irretrievably bound up in its setting; at one with the great oaks draped in Spanish moss, cypresses and sweet olives, all growing and thriving in the bayou's subtropical climate.

Until 1958, when the National Trust for Historic Preservation accepted the gift of the "Shadows," the house had never left the possession of the original Weeks family.

There is no escaping the drama and romance of Shadows-on-the-Teche. Its spirited beginning, its allegro middle years, its reluctant decline and now its nostalgic renascence hold in brick and mortar the memory of a long segment of Louisiana history. Part Grecian, part Anglo-American and part Creole — all of it mingled with a Gallic touch — the structure reflects the blending of architectural characteristics frequently seen in the great "statement" houses constructed when the nation was very young and very hopeful.

David Weeks, the builder of this grand house, was the son of one of the numerous Americans who migrated to the Creole Louisiana territory in search of fortune in the last years of Spanish domination, just prior to its purchase by the young republic in 1803. He left his father's successful plantation in the Feliciana region and sought his own future along the southern coast. In 1818, he met and married Mary Clara Conrad, and they purchased "Parc Perdu," a large plantation in the bayou country where three of their six children were born.

The next two decades were prosperous years in the delta, and David Weeks, as well as many other sugar planters in the region, began to build larger and grander residences that would reflect their newfound economic status. Acquiring property along the Bayou Teche, one of the many waterways flowing down to the Gulf of Mexico, the Weeks family began work on "Home Place," as the house was then called, near the small town of New Iberia in 1831. James Bedell, a master craftsman, was employed to design and build the house. Using clay scooped from the banks of the stream, bricks of a delicate coral coloration were produced on the plantation itself; cypress trees were cut, fashioned into massive timbers and set in place. Three years later, the Weeks family occupied their new home situated on a gentle bluff overlooking the Teche.

The exterior of the house owes its proportions to the Greek Revival mode of design. Eight columns of the Tuscan order stand firmly on low square bases, their shafts and capitals of brick and stucco. The entablature is classical, but here the architecture changes: the gabled slate roof, punctuated with three dormers on front and back, and the double-hung window sashes are of British-American origin. The interior is Louisiana French; three adjoining rooms meet across the front and back of the house, and there are no connecting halls or interior stairs. In typical Creole style, the rear rooms surround a *cabinet* gallery on three sides, and chimneys are built on interior wall spaces. The main stairway is located outside at one end of the front veranda or gallery and is a typical Louisiana arrangement: the staircase itself is shuttered from a front view, and a balancing lattice-motif has been installed at the opposite end of the gallery for symmetry.

David Weeks did not long enjoy the pleasures of his new plantation manor. Stricken with an ailment thought to be cancer, he died within a few months of his home's completion while on a trip to New Haven, Connecticut, to seek a cure for his malady and incidentally to select furnishings befitting the grand new house. Mary Clara Weeks later married Judge John Moore, a Louisiana congressman, and they divided their time between the political society of Washington and the planters' society of Louisiana. This influential Southern family, in their home on the Bayou Teche, enjoyed the last few decades of the glamorous antebellum era . . . a way of life that was soon to vanish.

Union forces marched into New Iberia during the Civil War, and the Union commander selected the Weeks-Moore residence for his headquarters. Though Mrs. Moore was seriously ill at the time, she courageously remained on her property to safeguard it from Federal confiscation. She died while officers were still occupying the house and was buried in her beloved garden.

In 1918, William Weeks Hall, a great-grandson of the original builder, acquired the house. Richard Koch, a New Orleans restoration architect and friend, supervised the transformation of the old place into a comfortable residence, adding a summer house in the garden. A confirmed bachelor, Hall entertained extensively during the 1930's and 1940's, and the house gained national fame as a focal point of literary and photographic works.

In failing health and concerned for the future of "Shadows," Hall began a 20-year quest starting in the 1930's to find a way to preserve the house and its garden setting. The National Trust for Historic Preservation responded favorably to his entreaty but would make no commitment until the gift of the house could be accompanied by a supporting endowment. Hall made deep personal sacrifices to amass the necessary funds. In 1958, just days before his death, he received word that the National Trust had accepted his bequest. A lifetime struggle to insure the beauty and dignity of "Shadows" had been requited. According to Hall's wishes, the house lives on as the embodiment of all that he and his ancestors envisioned for it.

FACING PAGE. *Standing amid moss-draped oaks, azaleas and gardenias is Shadows-on-the-Teche. The coral-colored, hand-made bricks and white Tuscan columns of this antebellum house blend into the semitropical landscape of New Iberia in southern Louisiana.*

ABOVE. *Adrian Persac, an artist, surveyor and mapmaker known for his maps of Louisiana parishes and the Mississippi River, probably sojourned at Shadows-on-the-Teche while painting two egg tempera views of the house in 1861. It is thought to be the only Louisiana home to boast front and back views executed by the artist.*

ABOVE. *Faithful to Weeks family letters, the bronze doré chandelier in the parlor is equipped with indigo-colored candles. The wooden spyglass on the Empire table may have belonged to William Weeks, the builder's father. A pair of bronze Argand lamps with crystal prisms is placed atop the marble mantel, and a portrait of Frances Weeks Magill Prewitt, daughter of the builder, hangs above.*

FACING PAGE. *Standing on a black and gray Italian marble floor is a Sheraton dining table set with Vieux Paris dinnerware, Sheffield gold-plated flatware and a silver cruet set by Kirk & Sons. The amber pitcher, water tumblers and wineglasses exhibit etched forest scenes. A Waterford crystal chandelier is reflected in the convex Regency mirror above the mantel. The silver chest, left, is by Duncan Phyfe, and the Adrian Persac painting of the Shadows is seen in the background.*

FACING PAGE. *The Sheraton bed is covered with a cotton Marseilles bedspread. A book-like, 19th century checker set is laid out on a Sheraton card table.*

ABOVE. *The tester bed in the master bedroom exhibits a massive cornice and octagonally faceted posts. The Sheraton mahogany armchair, upholstered in toile imprimée, features scrolled arms and turned front legs. A rosewood tester bed with Jacquard coverlet may be seen in the adjoining sitting room.*

LEFT. *A child's bedroom boasts a mahogany Sheraton tester bed with reeded posts and a melon headboard, a feature distinguishing it as Louisiana-made. David Weeks, the Shadows' builder, once owned the leather sea chest exhibiting brass beading and fittings. A homespun slave's vest is displayed on the chest. A tôle bath set and tin bathtub are shown at the right.*

147

ABOVE. *The summer house, built by architect Richard Koch for William Weeks Hall in 1928, was reconstructed in 1970 after a hurricane destroyed the original building.*

RIGHT. *Set amid 150-year-old live oaks, the antebellum home, seen from the rear, is an interesting blend of French Creole and Anglo-American architectural influences.*

PALMETTO HALL

Palmetto Hall, a mid-19th century testament to the heritage of Mobile, Alabama, is one of this port city's most breathtaking surprises. Shielded by live oaks and magnolia trees from the busy Spring Hill traffic outside its gates, the open-countenanced mansion stands at the apex of a formal circular drive in even greater splendor today than in its halcyon days before the Civil War.

The mansion's facade derives from the Greek Revival influence frequently interpreted impeccably in the antebellum South; the interior, however, has been completely redesigned with Neoclassical details. Sumptuously furnished to display collections of paintings and objects of art, nothing in Palmetto Hall's gleaming composure suggests the years of slumbering neglect the mansion suffered until it was reclaimed in 1963.

Palmetto Hall is a private residence, open to the public only on special occasions. A photographic record of the mansion is in the Historic American Buildings Survey on file in the Library of Congress.

The Mobile Historic Development Commission has traced the land on which Palmetto Hall was built to an 1827 deed of transfer from the United States government to William Richardson. This was 8 years after Alabama was admitted to the Union as the 22nd state and 13 years after Andrew Jackson defeated the Creek Indians, thus allowing access to the fertile bottom lands which produced cotton for the markets at Mobile and New Orleans.

The Richardson land passed to the William D. Cameron family and later to A.M. Barelli, who on June 8, 1850, conveyed a five-acre portion to Rose Earle Dawson. (Tradition has it that Palmetto Hall was built between 1846 and 1847 by Rose's husband, John C. Dawson, but since no legal records can be found to substantiate this earlier date, it is now thought that the house was constructed after the 1850 recorded land acquisition.)

The Dawson family had moved to Alabama from Charleston, and although their new home displayed John Dawson's growing affluence as a successful Mobile merchant, he paid homage to his South Carolina origins by naming his palatial hall "Palmetto" after the state tree of South Carolina.

The foundation and ground level of Palmetto Hall are stucco over masonry; the second story is of frame construction. In the manner of many coastal dwellings, an exterior staircase at one time led to a second-story central entry, which opened onto a wide hall, with large rooms on either side used for family living and entertaining. The first story was used to house the more utilitarian rooms such as kitchen, storage areas and informal dining rooms.

The house remained in the Dawson family until 1919, when it was sold by Hanna H. Dawson to Lola G. George. It passed from Mrs. George's hands to Joseph T. McKeon in 1922 and remained in his family until 1960, when it was purchased by the present owners.

Since a hurricane in 1906 had damaged the original exterior staircase and other major portions of Palmetto Hall, the owners employed the professional help of New Orleans architect Myrlin McCullar to revive the fine old home and plan its elaborate regeneration. As a result, although many of the architectural details were retained, the original rather severe style has been changed to that of an impressive Palladian villa.

The two-story central block is enlarged by symmetrical offset wings, and a two-story porch now extends the full width of the main block. Articulated by Doric columns, the double-colonnade porch is five bays wide by one bay deep. The first-story columns are unfluted circular plaster shafts with square plinths, torus molded bases and a strong molding below the capitals. The second story has slender Doric columns, fluted, with a continuous balustrade of delicate design. Typical of the Greek Revival style, the main roof is invisible from ground view, hidden behind the cornice which continues around the building beneath the house eaves; the one-story wings have hip roofs.

Window and door arrangements on the first floor have been altered and bear no resemblance to the original design. The main double-door entrance, now on the ground level, is Greek Revival in style and simpler than the second-story Federal entrance with its semicircular transom that extends the width of the door and sidelights.

These exterior architectural modifications, however, are only part of the story of Palmetto Hall's new life. Inside, the rooms are palatial. The expanded ground level two-story atrium foyer opens to a curving freestanding staircase with a balustraded, elongated octagonal balcony supported from below by Corinthian columns. At the head of the stairs, somewhat smaller columns flank double doors leading into an upstairs bedroom. A ballroom, with marble floors, a carved marble fireplace, heavy moldings and enough space to entertain 200 guests, is located on the ground level.

The furnishings in the formal dining room, loggia and cross-hall are impressive: Biedermeier, English, French and signed American Empire case pieces and cabinetry; Bristol and Waterford chandeliers; Directoire Aubusson, Savonnerie, Heriz and Tabriz carpets and a collection of bronze doré by Pierre-Philippe Thomire. The formal drawing room contains one of Palmetto Hall's greatest treasures. Standing majestically against cypress-paneled walls is a magnificient book cabinet, circa 1750, fashioned by the incomparable English craftsman William Vile. Its superbly carved bonnet complements the carvings that embellish the room's overdoors and overmantel, which were executed by Grinling Gibbons, an associate of Sir Christopher Wren. In the Federal or Sword room, a small collection of American presentation swords, set with gold, silver and precious stones, is displayed, while a gathering of malachite and gold objects, graces an Empire table in the back cross-hall.

Commanding focal points throughout the house are portraits and landscapes by some of America's finest artists: Gilbert Stuart, Rembrandt Peale, Thomas Sully, Frederic Remington, Charles Peale Polk, James Henry Beard, John Singer Sargent, William Aiken Walker.

Palmetto Hall's house and gardens have received the Historic Mobile Preservation Society Architectural Award for restoration.

PRECEDING PAGE. *Palmetto Hall is a Southern mansion built in 1850 near the gulf shores of Mobile, Alabama. The house is distinguished by six Tuscan columns standing on a piazza of old brick. These support the upper gallery which has six fluted Doric columns joined by a delicate banister railing.*

LEFT. *In the drawing room is an array of fine English antique furniture and portraits by celebrated American artists. A superbly carved breakfront by early George III cabinet-maker William Vile highlights the collection. Regency torchères on each side of the breakfront balance with ornately carved overdoors and overmantel by Grinling Gibbons. The mantel, inlaid with pewter, is American, the chandelier is Bristol, and the rug is a signed Kerman. Portrait of Esther Cox Binney, above the mantel, is by Thomas Sully. The other portraits are by Rembrandt Peale, James Peale and an unidentified Southern Louisiana painter.*

RIGHT. *Displayed on an Empire table in the cross-hall is a portion of an extensive collection of malachite and gold masterworks belonging to the homeowner. Oil paintings above the table and chairs are representative of the large assemblage of American landscape paintings in the house.*

BELOW. *A Directoire Aubusson carpet of enormous proportion covers the marble floor of the ballroom. An exceptionally fine collection of Americana including portraits by Charles Peale Polk, James Henry Beard and Thomas Sully, a landscape by F.A. Butman, a Bennetter seascape and rare American Empire furniture is exhibited in the room. An épergne by leading English Regency silversmith, Paul Storr (1771-1844) distinguishes the center table.*

156

ABOVE. *Centering the William IV banquet table is a gilded bronze, mirrored plateau holding a collection of bronze doré pieces created by French Empire metal chaser and engraver, Pierre-Philippe Thomire. Chairs are English Regency. A Worcester "Flight & Barr" dinner service, circa 1791, is contained in the Chippendale breakfront. Portrait on the right is of Zachary Taylor, 12th President of the United States, by James Henry Beard.*

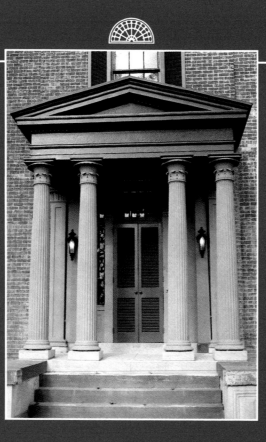

GLENWOOD

Glenwood, a stately house built in the 1850's, is situated on a knoll surrounded by elms, sycamores and magnolia trees. It was located in the countryside west of the Elk River on outlying farmland adjacent to Charleston, West Virginia. Although rural in setting, there were few homes of the day that could match its formal sophistication.

Charleston's West Side residential neighborhood has now reached out to encircle Glenwood, but the house still retains its original aloof beauty and dignity; the classical conception of its builder has not been altered. Only the color of the bricks and wood trim differs from the original, a step taken so long ago that it is barely perceptible.

Built by James Madison Laidley in the years preceding the Civil War, Glenwood was purchased by George Summers II only five years after its completion. Under the capable stewardship of the Summers family it has been passed from generation to generation and is still as it was throughout the 19th century.

Thirteen years before West Virginia achieved its severence from the Old Dominion and became a state, James Madison Laidley, an attorney from Parkersburg, moved to Charleston in western Virginia.

This community on the banks of the Kanawha River was a bustling town of 1500 citizens when the newly arrived lawyer first established and became editor of the *Western Register*. A born entrepreneur, Laidley was also involved in the thriving business of salt-making, the Kanawha Valley's principal industry, and using the profits garnered from his several enterprises, he was able to buy 366 acres of rich farmland across the Elk River from Charleston. Accessible by ferry, with an uninterrupted view of both the river and the town of Charleston beyond, his home was named Glenwood after its arcadian environment near a rocky cove and waterfall.

Mr. Laidley spared no expense in the construction of his new home. Under the direction of William Preston, an English stonemason and builder, materials indigenous to the area were incorporated in the structure by utilizing brick fired at a nearby kiln, sandstone for the ashlar block foundation from a neighboring quarry and walnut from bordering groves for the decorative trim. But while the materials were native to the area, the result was clearly urbane and refined. The house was built in the Greek Revival style, and delicately wrought pairs of Corinthian columns and a dentil cornice gave distinction to the well-proportioned exterior.

No less interesting than the main house is a structure known as "the Quarters," a four-room brick outbuilding reached by a cobblestone courtyard from the galleries across the rear of the mansion. Predating the main structure by two years, it was used as a temporary dwelling by the Laidleys while Glenwood was under construction. Throughout the 19th century, the kitchen was located in the Quarters, and food was carried to the main house by servants. When the meal was finished, water was carried across to the dining room, where the fine china was carefully washed right at the dining room table.

Laidley, with his wife Anna Beuhring Laidley and their large family of children, lived at Glenwood for only five years. Although no reason is known for their decision to move to smaller lodgings elsewhere, it has been surmised that the family's straitened circumstances, due to a decline in salt prices and a widespread depression in 1857, may have necessitated this change in their lifestyle.

Glenwood was later sold to George W. Summers II, one of western Virginia's most distinguished figures. He had served in the Virginia state legislature and also in Congress. A dynamic speaker, he was involved in conferences aimed at the conciliation of differences between the peoples of eastern Virginia and those of the western mountain region who would, in 1863, vote to become the inhabitants of the new state of West Virginia. Summers remained politically active until it became evident that civil war was inevitable. A political moderate who had hoped that conflict could be avoided, George Summers retreated from public life to his private law practice and his secluded home on the Elk River.

When war came to the Kanawha Valley, shells aimed from the hills across the river rained down on the estate. Despite the successive occupancies of both the Confederate and Union armies, Glenwood escaped virtually unscathed. As a result of that unhappy conflict, however, a personal loss of another and more tragic kind touched George and his wife, Amacetta. A child bride at the age of 16, Amacetta had borne 13 children, only two of whom, both boys, had survived beyond childhood. The war claimed the elder son, George Summers III, and only Lewis Summers II was left to inherit Glenwood at his parents' deaths a few years later.

Lewis and his bride Ludy Woodbridge moved into the house in 1868. As they crossed the threshold for the first time, they continued a tradition begun by Amacetta Summers . . . a Bible and a small measure of salt were carried into the house, a ritual to bless the new dwelling place and its occupants. Cast in the role of gentleman farmer, Lewis Summers soon found such a large property no longer serviceable in a changing society, and he sold all of the vast estate but an acre and three quarters.

His son and heir Lewis Summers III had no surviving children, and at his death, his nieces, Lucy and Elizabeth Quarrier, the great-granddaughters of George and Amacetta Summers, became owners of Glenwood in 1953. Both had been born at Glenwood. There they had mounted their horses under the front entrance portico; and there they had entertained their young friends. So it was with great nostalgic pleasure that they undertook its renovation. Working with Mrs. Gene Pennypacker of Winchester, Virginia, they restored Glenwood to its mid-19th century elegance. After refurbishing the interior, the new owners took equal delight in recreating and designing the flower and herb gardens attached to the house. Now listed on the National Register of Historic Places, Glenwood has been deeded to the West Virginia College of Graduate Studies Foundation providing a focus for artisans and scholars interested in native crafts.

That this mellow and gracious home continues to speak for itself is a happy circumstance. Few houses of its antebellum character exist in the Kanawha Valley area. Best of all, Glenwood's integrity has been most beautifully preserved, an enduring legacy for future generations to cherish.

FACING PAGE. *Overlooking the Elk River near Charleston, West Virginia, stands Glenwood, a fine old house built in 1852. The entrance portico, with pairs of reeded Corinthian columns and pilasters on either side of the door, presents a demeanor of both strength and grace.*

ABOVE. *The entrance foyer holds a collection of important American antiques among which are an American Sheraton-style long-case clock, circa 1810, made by Jesse Woltz; two bridge-whist tables, circa 1820, made in the style of Duncan Phyfe and a mahogany sofa of American Empire design, circa 1845. A portrait of Judge Lewis Summers, attributed to George Catlin, hangs to the left.*

FACING PAGE. *The American Empire-style mahogany sideboard holds the Repoussé silver tea service by Kirk. The three-section American Sheraton-Directoire cherry dining table can accommodate 20 people when fully extended. The chairs are American Empire, circa 1830.*

ABOVE. *At home in the master bedroom is the walnut high-post bed, a mid-19th century piece. The cherry chest with glass pulls, American Sheraton in design is mid-19th century.*

LEFT. *The square, rosewood grand piano in the parlor was a gift to Amacetta Summers from her husband George Summers, second owners of the house. Their portraits, painted by George Caleb Bingham hang on either side of an ornate gilt and wood mirror.*

ABOVE. *The two-story outbuilding known as the "Quarters" was built in 1850 to house the James Madison Laidley family while the mansion was being constructed. The structure was recently restored under the guidance of Charleston architect Paul Marshall, AIA.*

RIGHT. *For many years food was prepared here in the Quarters' kitchen and carried to the main house. While restoring this room, the random-width planks were taken up, unearthing chards of pottery and the china head of a doll. All of the furniture is old.*

DUNLEITH

Beginning in 1716, the flags of five major powers have at various times been raised over the site of Natchez, Mississippi. Influenced by the heritage of these separate cultures, Natchez is an astonishing national archive, as valiantly marked by time and circumstance as any city in the country. Thirty antebellum mansions set down in this historic milieu reflect the spirit of Southern Colonial and Greek Revival architecture.

In the flourishing years before the Confederacy, a group of hard-driving Natchez planters harvested vast fortunes from their cotton fields and built glorious monuments to their prosperity and manner of life. Dunleith is a recognized signature of those times . . . the Golden Age of the South.

Situated on 40 acres of green pastures and wooded bayous, Dunleith has been honored by the Southern Heritage Society for its architectural grace and beauty. Dunleith is listed on the National Register of Historic Places and is a National Historic Landmark. Now owned by Mr. and Mrs. William F. Heins III, the mansion's sumptuously furnished lower floor is open to the public.

Located on a high cliff overlooking the Mississippi River, Natchez endured long years of territorial conquest before demand for cotton set its antebellum commerce humming in the early 1800's.

The Natchez Indians bequeathed their name to the area and were the first to covet the 200-foot bluff above the rampaging waters of the Mississippi. Then, as early as 1682, the French explorer La Salle, floating downstream in search of the mighty river's mouth, realized that strategic control of this vital water way lay in commanding the heights above; in 1716, the French established Fort Rosalie on the bluffs, and after the bloody French and Indian War, Britain stepped in and raised the Union Jack over the settlement. Through subsequent lavish land grants to British officers, the crown set the pattern for big holdings and privileged wealth. The area became Britain's "14th colony." During England's conflict with her colonies on the Eastern seacoast, Spain quietly moved in to assert its claim to the Natchez territory. But by 1798, following the close of the American Revolution, the Spanish dons reluctantly relinquished control.

Early in the 1800's, settlement of the area was spurred by the lure of cotton lands, and the next decades of bustling activity demonstrated the unparalleled success of King Cotton. Around 1850, Natchez could boast of more millionaires than any city except New York.

Job Routh, one of the more successful cotton kings, built the first manor house on the Dunleith site. Having parceled out portions of his 1700-acre holding to other children, he gave his own home, Routhland, to his daughter Mary and her second husband Charles Dahlgren, a fiery-tempered man and a direct descendant of Sweden's King Gustavus Adolphus. In 1845, while the couple was in residence, Routhland burned to the ground. In a letter, Dahlgren later stated ". . . it was struck by lightning and destroyed, in consequence of my wife desiring terra cotta chimney tops placed, which were elevated above the surrounding china trees, and so affording an object for electric fluid." The Dahlgrens rebuilt, completing the present house in 1856. Three years later, they sold it to Alfred V. Davis, who changed its name to Dunleith.

The Civil War saw a curious incident at the mansion. Davis raised thoroughbred horses, and one day, according to the story, he learned that Union officers were on their way to his home to requisition his stock. In an an attempt to retain some of these prized animals, he decided to hide his best horses in the cellar beneath the dining room. After the officers arrived and surveyed his stables, he invited them to dine with him. Fortunately, the concealed horses made no sound during the meal, and Davis' sangfroid was rewarded.

During the Civil War, Natchez yielded to the advancing Union troops and was spared the fate of many other Southern towns, and throughout the 19th century, the city continued to be wealthy and important.

Dunleith changed hands several times until it was acquired by Joseph N. Carpenter in 1886. The mansion remained in the Carpenter family for the next four generations. In 1976, Mr. and Mrs. William F. Heins III of Conroe, Texas, bought Dunleith and restored and refurbished it.

The entire lower floor of Dunleith is open to the public. Visitors enter through a wide entrance hall which runs the depth of the house, with two spacious rooms on each side. To the left of the entrance are magnificent double drawing rooms furnished with pieces dating 1850 or earlier; soft shades of yellow, pink and green tie these rooms together. In the library on the right, a rich blue cotton satin covers the walls. The adjacent dining room is adorned with French Zuber wallpaper printed before World War I from woodblocks carved in 1855.

The second floor, architecturally the same as the first, is reserved as living quarters. A staircase winds to the third floor which has, again, four rooms, with a fireplace in each.

The Heins' latest restoration is the 18-room servants' quarters attached to the house. This wing houses a mid-1850's plumbing system, coal room and a meat storage room complete with hooks for hanging game. On the terrace behind it is a poultry house topped by a pigeonnier.

Dunleith is part of the Natchez Spring and Fall Pilgrimages. The Heins have established a horticulture program which provides color for the spacious grounds year around.

LEFT. *Surrounded by 40 acres of green pastures and woodlands, Dunleith, an imposing Greek Revival mansion, stands renewed on a rise near the heart of Natchez. Built in 1855, it is the only example to be found on the Mississippi today of an antebellum residence that is encircled by Doric columns and double-tiered galleries. Often called the most photographed house in the South, it has been cited by the Southern Heritage Society for its architectural grace and beauty.*

ABOVE. *A wide gallery, interrupted by massive white columns and delicate wrought iron, borders the symmetrical structure on all sides.*

ABOVE. *A broad center hallway with original pine floors runs the depth of the house with two spacious rooms on each side. Centered on a rosewood English Regency table is an antique Sèvres urn with ormolu mounts and painted panels. The breakfront and settees are English.*

FACING PAGE. *Above the marble fireplace in the library hangs a large 18th century Italian painting. The gossip, or corner chair, is English, circa 1760, and the marble-top bookcase is English Regency, 1815.*

FACING PAGE. *The magnificent double drawing room is resplendent with antiques dating from the 1850's. In days past, ladies retired after dinner to one of the double parlors for tea, while the men enjoyed cigars and brandy in the other. A Napoleon II, French cylinder desk, signed "F. Durand & Sons," in the rose parlor features marquetry inlay of kingwood, satinwood and ebony and has exceptional gold doré plaques and mounts.*

ABOVE. *In the center of the yellow parlor is a table signed by Linke. Old Paris porcelain compote, circa 1820, and French bronze and gold doré candelabra with winged figures, circa 1810, grace the mantel of the Italian marble fireplace. Mirrors and chandeliers are French.*

The Italian sienna marble fireplace in the dining room is original to the room. French wallpaper is a Zuber scenic printed sometime before World War I, in tempera color from the original woodblocks made in 1855. This wallpaper is extremely difficult to execute and is believed to have been printed only twice. The late 19th century American table, chairs, buffet and server are mahogany inlaid with satinwood. Chandelier and matching candelabra, circa 1815, are Waterford crystal.

VILLA FINALE

Villa Finale, the former Norton-Polk-Mathis house in San Antonio, Texas, is all curves and arches, light and shadow, subtle friezes and romantic recesses, a joyous dome of pleasure, with only the sound of cathedral bells from its balustraded and crowned Italian Renaissance tower offering a sobering hint of melancholy.

It could have been the castle of a Genoan doge, the fanciful palace of an Ottoman sultan or the stronghold of a Mediterranean buccaneer, but it stands instead with bravura in the heart of San Antonio, proudly reminiscent of the empire of the old cattle barons.

San Antonio was a lusty cowtown in 1876 when the coming of the railroad to south central Texas opened unparalleled opportunities for trade development. Completed the same year, the mansion was built by Russell Norton, a prosperous merchant, and subsequently belonged to three legendary families associated with the cattle trails: the Polks, the Pryors and the Fants.

Villa Finale has been brought back to its original exuberance as an example of cosmopolitan taste and is one of the centerpieces in San Antonio's King William district.

The home was only 93 years old, a modest age for great houses, but the proud structure was rapidly declining to ruin when it was acquired in 1969 by the present owner, Walter Nold Mathis. Neglected throughout the first half of the 20th century, this old and crumbling relic was recognized by the Texas Historic Commission as the Norton-Polk-Mathis house.

A native Texan and descendant of early settlers from the Canary Islands, Mr. Mathis was an investment banker who had a consuming passion and a magic touch for aesthetic regeneration. He acquired and reclaimed a total of 14 homes in the King William section of San Antonio, a monumental and successful restoration project. In 1968, this entire area was designated a historic district, and it is now listed on the National Register of Historic Places.

The prima donna of the King William restorations . . . the Norton-Polk-Mathis house . . . Mr. Mathis chose to keep for himself. His imagination, quickened by the buoyant spirit of the home's history and architectural interest, led him to recreate the original setting as a repository for the significant and valuable treasures he assembled with his collector's eye. He renamed his house "Villa Finale" . . . ultimate home.

The story of this transformation begins in the colorful and unstructured cattlemen's heyday of the 1870's. Russell Norton, the original builder, was a prosperous hardware merchant. Undaunted by the lack of any formal architectural training, he began construction of a house that was Italianate in flavor, combining his own ideas of structural suitability with lightness of ornamentation and detail. The house was built by German stonemasons of strong, native Texas limestone quarried near Fredericksburg. It boasts intricately carved capitals and friezes, impressive entablatures and heavily accented cornices. A front two-story balcony has four soft oval arches outlining the lower loggia, balanced on the top story with four rectangles separated by slender columns of a neo-Ionic order. Windows were proportionately shaped: strong rectangles in the principal rooms, long, slender apertures in small chambers, ovals and rounds where they would be proper.

It is not certain whether much of this unconventional opulence was original to Mr. Norton's designs or whether it was added after possession of the house passed through an extraordinary succession of flamboyant and legendary cattle barons. These were all men to be reckoned with in the early days of San Antonio society, and it is not hard to imagine the indelible imprint such free-wheeling and determined men of action would leave on any home they occupied. What is known for certain is that time, hard use and neglect had all taken their toll when Walter Mathis first undertook the restoration of this historic mansion.

Although the original mantels remained intact, there were eight fireplaces to be repaired. Nine stained glass windows, discovered in the basement, were releaded and rehung in their original openings. Four wood-burning stoves were put back into useful operation. Cypress shutters were mended or replaced, as was much of the woodwork. The limestone was steam-cleaned to remove layers of paint from the capitals and friezes. The detailed plasterwork, especially notable in the double parlor, was restored, and the light gold-stenciled border above the chair rail in the downstairs hall and parlor was brilliantly reoutlined.

This patient restoration of Villa Finale took more than a year to complete. The house is now furnished with exquisite period pieces, European art and decorative objects of great variety, including a valuable collection of Napoleonic artifacts of silver, bronze, ivory and wood. An extensive silver collection is on display, and several of the rooms have been furnished with family heirlooms and Texas-made objects, including memorabilia recalling early frontier days. A kitchen in the basement is still used for cooking on special occasions and another basement area is used primarily as a game room.

The landscaping at Villa Finale owes much of its scenic beauty to Mr. Mathis. A devoted horticulturist, he designed and created the formal boxwood garden to complement the south side of the house. Elsewhere his design draws the eye irresistibly eastward toward the banks of the San Antonio River; here the grounds are devoted exclusively to such native trees as anaqua, red oak, pecan, magnolia and elm.

Villa Finale has been described in several publications over the years, the first on record being *Harpers Monthly Magazine* in 1877. More than 100 years later, in the September 1979, issue of *Antiques,* Elisabeth Donaghy Garrett wrote this appropriate addendum: "The handsome elegance of Villa Finale evokes the halcyon days of King William Street at the end of the 19th century, but its easy elegance belies the labor and dedication required to restore the house to its early state." As the name implies, Villa Finale has become the ultimate abode . . . an early Texas achievement where memories of the 19th century have been recaptured enabling a new dream to come true.

FACING PAGE. *Villa Finale, one of the most palatial residences in the King William District of San Antonio, Texas, was begun in 1876 for a prominent hardware merchant. The Italianate house, acquired in 1969 by Walter Nold Mathis, is set amid manicured lawns that extend to the San Antonio River.*

ABOVE. *A grand center hall divides the library and dining room from the double parlor. An elaborate gold stenciled border above the chair rail that continues around the double parlor and extends up the stairwell has been restored. The stained glass window at the landing is one of nine restored for Mr. Mathis.*

ABOVE. *The north, double parlor contains a collection of French Empire furniture, including desk, side chairs and armchairs. Early 19th century Sèvres vases rest on a pair of encoignures marked Lesage, a well-known Parisian furniture store of the 19th century.*

RIGHT. *Silver, ivory, bronze and wooden figures of Napoleon arranged on a table are but a small portion of Mr. Mathis' collection of Napoleonic objects. The portrait of Napoleon above the table was painted during his lifetime.*

FACING PAGE. *An air of sophistication characterizes the dining room, which holds an English chandelier, American mahogany chairs and French overmantel mirror. A silver-gilt épergne on a mirrored plateau ornaments the center of the table. Matching fruit bowls decorated with silver sphinxes and camels stand on either side. A silver tea service enriches the English side table, above which hangs a painting of St. Cecilia executed in the manner of Michelangelo Merisi da Caravaggio.*

ABOVE. *The north sitting room on the second floor has a circular stair leading to a bedroom. The rococo revival settee and chairs were purchased in New Orleans. A French settee stands in the foreground.*

RIGHT. *The Renaissance revival bedroom suite was purchased by Mr. Mathis' grandfather in Cincinnati in 1870 for his Rockport, Texas, residence. Groupings of photographs of Mr. Mathis' ancestors are attractively arranged on each side of the bed.*

WHITEHALL

In the Florida of the late 1880's, Henry Morrison Flagler was undoubtedly the most prescient and significant man of his time, and "Whitehall," his Spanish-Colonial castle at Palm Beach was built to reflect his success. It was also planned as a wedding present for his third wife, the gracious and accomplished Mary Lily Kenan of North Carolina.

The turn of the 20th century was the pinnacle of south Florida's evolution from a sand and marshland backwater to a flourishing mecca of white beaches and tropical landscapes. It was a grand epoch which saw the extension of a railroad to Key West, the dredging of Miami Harbor, the establishment of steamship lines, the development of palatial hotels and a network of community improvements — all the work of H. M. Flagler.

Henry Flagler had been star-touched from the day he left Hopewell, New York, in 1844 as a boy of 14 with nine cents and a French coin. By his early twenties, thanks to superb business acumen and hard work, he had established a business in the salt market and amassed a fortune. Undaunted by subsequent bankruptcy, he repaid every debt with interest and went on to make a second fortune in the grain business. He later joined with John D. Rockefeller and other investors in organizing the Standard Oil Company.

Already pre-eminent in the nation's loftiest industrial and financial circles, Flagler came to Florida for the health of his first wife, Mary Harkness Flagler. After her death in 1881, he remained for the adventure and challenge. He completed the first in a series of projects, the fabulous Ponce de Leon Hotel in St. Augustine, at the age of 58.

For the next two and one-half decades, Flagler was Florida, and Florida was Flagler: he constructed hotels, towns (West Palm Beach), churches, docks and wharves and formed a steamship line serving Key West and nearby Caribbean islands. In an amazing feat of engineering and tenacity, Flagler connected Key West by rail with mainland Florida, a struggle that took seven years and cost some $20,000,000. The House of Morgan called Flagler a genius and appraised his Florida East Coast railway extension as "a more marvelous achievement than similar developments anywhere else in the world."

Flagler married again, but was divorced. In 1901, at the age of 71, he took a third wife, Miss Mary Lily Kenan of Kenansville, North Carolina. Shortly thereafter — as an expression of his "contentment" — he commissioned the construction of the "white palace" as a wedding gift. Whitehall stands on a six-acre site bordering Lake Worth. Designed by New York architects John M. Carrère and Thomas Hastings, both of whom had studied at the Ecole des Beaux-Arts in France, the mansion is shielded from the street by a wrought-iron fence with stunning arched double gates. The landscaped approach through coconut palms and orange trees leads to an imposing three-story stucco building with a red-tiled roof and heavy Doric columns across the facade. Designed in the manner of Spanish palaces, the rooms enclose a tropical courtyard, and a promenade leads from each ground-level room to the central garden. The centerpiece of the courtyard is a Bathing Venus fountain, a copy of the original in the Boboli Gardens in Florence, Italy, executed by Gioavanni da Bologna in 1584.

The real glory of Whitehall, however, is its interior design and ornamentations. At an estimated cost of $1,500,000 at the turn of the century, William P. Stymus, Jr., of the New York firm of Pottier and Stymus, gathered opulent furnishings and fixtures from all over the world. The names of the rooms are an indication of their variety and decor: an Italian Renaissance library, a Louis XIV music room, a Swiss billiard room, a Louis XV ballroom and a Francis I dining room. The dimensions are gigantic: the marble Entrance Hall is 110' x 40'; the main ballroom is 91' x 37', and the smallest room on the ground floor, the Elizabethan breakfast room, is 23' x 21'. On the second floor, in addition to the master suite and sitting room, there are fourteen guest chambers on the east side, most with individual baths and dressing rooms. On the west side there are thirteen servants rooms; the third level was reserved for maids and valets brought in for special events.

The most sumptuous materials that could be found were incorporated into Whitehall: seven varieties of marble, including Pavanazza and Carrara; domed and arched ceilings with painted canvas ceiling panels and papier-mâché insets molded in Limoges, France; carpets from Kerman, Savonnerie and English Axminster; rare Aubusson tapestries, Rose du Barry silk damasks and velvets; sculptures; crystal and bronze doré chandeliers; museum quality appointments; paintings by Gainsborough, Romney, Canaletto, Detti, Frangiamore, Schreyer and Louis Comfort Tiffany; exquisite porcelains; the largest pipe organ ever installed in a private home; a 39-pound English silver punch-bowl; and such endearing and intimate touches as a collection of family Bibles and a pianola in the music room.

Usually open only for the winter season when it required a full complement of twenty-one servants, Whitehall was planned for magnificent parties and hospitality. A newspaper clipping acclaimed Flagler's residence as the "most beautiful house in the Far South," and described a party honoring George Washington's birthday "as the most brilliant of Southern social gatherings."

When Mr. and Mrs. Flagler died, Whitehall was sold by their niece, Louise Wise Lewis, to a group of investors. Briefly converted into a private club and then a luxury hotel in 1925, the mansion was purchased in 1959 by the Henry Morrison Flagler Museum under the leadership of Jean Flagler Matthews, Henry Flagler's granddaughter. The museum was opened in 1960 and the public can now see what *The New York Herald* could only describe to its readers in 1902 ". . . there is nothing in the world to equal Whitehall. When the doors are opened to guests, Mrs. Flagler can bid her friends welcome to a home which, in point of grandeur, queen or princess never knew."

PRECEDING PAGE. *Whitehall was built in 1901 by Henry Morrison Flagler as a wedding gift for his bride, Mary Lily Kenan. It was designed by two young architects, John M. Carrére and Thomas Hastings in the Beaux-Arts style. Although this style was most often seen in public buildings, by the end of the century it was being adapted for town houses and resort villas.*
LEFT. *Walls, floors and columns of the 110 foot long, 40 foot wide entrance hall are made of seven different varieties of marble. Massive benches and urns on either side of the stairway*

are of carved Carrara marble. Large gold armchairs are Louis XIV style and the painted canvas ceiling panels and dome are attributed to the Italian artist Benvenuti.
ABOVE. *The French salon is resplendent with gray painted boiserie embellished with silver gilt. Brocatelle draperies and lace curtains accompany the softly painted sky of the ceiling medallion which is rife with cherubs. Carved white marble mantel with silver facings and gilt furnishings in 18th century French styles complete the elegant setting.*

FACING PAGE. *16th century Italian Renaissance styles are reflected in the satin grained walnut paneling and carved and gilded woodwork of the dining room. The mantelpiece, carved with garlands of fruit and sea motifs is surmounted by a portrait of Louis XIV. Gilt and walnut grained plaster ceiling is inset with papier mâché made and molded in Limoges, France.*

ABOVE. *Walls of the Italian Renaissance library, decorated according to early 16th century styles, is paneled in Circassian walnut and hung with red Spanish silk damask. Walnut chairs, Chinese porcelain incense burner and andirons are original to the house.*

LEFT. *Plaster beamed ceiling in the billiard room is grained to resemble the oak of the wainscoting. Mantel, window and door surrounds are of French Caen stone. An English skittles table stands between billiard and pool tables.*